MEDIEVAL NEEDLEPOINT

MEDIEVAL NEEDLEPOINT

Twenty-four easy-to-make
projects for the home

Debby Robinson

Sterling Publishing Co., Inc. New York

Edited and designed by Collins & Brown Limited
Editorial Director: Gabrielle Townsend
Editor: Sarah Bloxham
Art Director: Roger Bristow
Designed by: Ruth Hope

Filmset by Goodfellow & Egan, Cambridge
Reproduction by J. Film, Bangkok, Thailand

Library of Congress Cataloging-in-Publication Data Available

2 4 6 8 10 9 7 5 3 1

Published in 1993 by Sterling Publishing Company, Inc.
387 Park Avenue South, New York, N.Y. 10016
Originally published in Great Britain by Collins & Brown Limited
Mercury House, 195 Knightsbridge, London SW7 1RE
Copyright © 1992 by Collins & Brown Limited
Text copyright © 1992 Debby Robinson
Designs copyright © 1992 Debby Robinson
Distributed in Canada by Sterling Publishing
c/o Canadian Manda Group, P. O. Box 920, Station U
Toronto, Ontario, Canada M8Z 5P9
Printed and Bound in Italy
All rights reserved

Sterling ISBN 0-8069-8820-7

Edited and designed by Collins & Brown Limited
Editorial Director: Gabrielle Townsend
Editor: Sarah Bloxham
Art Director: Roger Bristow
Designed by: Ruth Hope
Project stitching by: Jillian Taylor, Needle Needs Ltd
Project photography by: Geoff Dann
Line drawings by: Kate Simunek

Filmset by Goodfellow & Egan, Cambridge
Reproduction by J. Film, Bangkok, Thailand
Printed and bound in Italy

The medieval source pictures are reproduced by kind permission of the
following: Biblioteca Laurenziana, Florence (Bridgeman Art Library) 33;
Bibliothèque Nationale, Paris (Bridgeman Art Library) 21, 81, 105, 113;
Bodleian Library, Oxford (Bridgeman Art Library) 71; The British
Library 9 (Bridgeman Art Library) 41, 93; Christ Church College,
Oxford (Wake Collection) 27; Keble College, Oxford (Woodmansterne
Library) 63; Musée de Bayeux (Michael Holford) 10; Musée Condé,
Chantilly (Bridgeman Art Library) 13, 45; Sir John Soane Museum,
London (ET Archive) 87, 99; Victoria & Albert Museum, London
(ET Archive) 49, 109.

Contents

Introduction

WHEN I WAS FIRST ASKED to create a collection of needlepoint designs using medieval illuminated manuscripts as inspiration I actually thought it might prove to be a difficult task finding enough references which would happily translate into stitchery. The difficulty, however, was in choosing only twenty-four designs from the gloriously rich world held within their pages. I was to spend many an afternoon surrounded by boxes of photographic transparencies simply revelling in the beautiful images, never mind doing any serious work as to suitability, detail, colour matching, and so on.

Although the main scene depicted in many manuscripts would have been impossible to recreate in needlepoint, the borders provided me with an incredibly varied source of material. It was here that the artist's imagination could run riot and it is here that flourishes of style are to be found. Stunningly realistic animals and insects often inhabit the same tangle of leaves, fruit and flowers as fantastic grotesques from the realms of mythology. My researches with the magnifying glass became rather like a nature trek as I discovered the beasts and botanic specimens of centuries ago, long since painted but still glowing with vibrant colour.

Many of these pigments cannot be accurately recreated in wool as they were made from precious materials, such as ground lapis lazuli, which produced colours of a unique intensity. It was therefore very difficult to do some of the original colours justice when using a modern palette, despite the wonderful range of coloured threads available. I also had to ensure that each design used a group of colours that was harmonious, rather than going for exact individual colour matches.

There is a charming idiosyncrasy to medieval illumination. Even a border that appears symmetrical will be far from it. It is as if each design developed organically, progressing over the page unhampered by any rules. For this reason I often had to tamper with the composition in the interests of balance, especially since I was frequently extracting only a very small area from the whole. Artistic devices or little creatures often popped up out of the blue for no apparent reason except, possibly, to cover a paint blot on the vellum all those years ago.

When my final choices were made many lovely examples had to be rejected for technical reasons and also to provide a set of designs which would be varied in intricacy, scale, colour and subject matter. From these I hope that I have succeeded in creating an interesting and attractive group of projects which will not only appeal in their own right but will give you inspiration to experiment and produce needlepoint of your own design as unique as a medieval painting.

Debby Robinson
London, 1992

These chair seat covers capture the richness of the medieval palette;
blue, red and gold were the most expensive and precious pigments
available to the illuminator.

The Medieval Heritage

'Flowers, plants, fishes, beasts, birds, flies, and bees,
Hills, dales, plains, pastures, skies, seas, rivers, trees;
There's nothing near at hand, or farthest sought,
But with the needle may be shaped and wrought.'

The Needle's Excellency, JOHN TAYLER

I N THIS BOOK, the motifs and designs used as decorative detail by the illuminators of medieval manuscripts have been reinterpreted for the modern-day worker in needlepoint.

Many of these manuscripts were religious in theme—Gospels, Psalters and Books of Hours, meant as aids to private devotion—so the decorative element was confined to the margins, while the main image was often a biblical scene. Manuscript production was practically a Church monopoly and all early medieval manuscripts were written and illustrated by monks working in the scriptoria of monasteries. Later, however, books were just as likely to be produced for laymen as for clergy, and these were mainly illuminated by masters working independently of the religious foundations, men such as the Boucicault Master, whose work can be seen on page 21. These later works often took more secular themes, being copies of pagan, classical texts from ancient Greece and Rome, such as the *Dialogues* of Plato and Virgil's *Aeneid*, or of medieval histories and romances.

But whatever the book's subject, it was not made just to be read; it was also meant to be given. Rare and precious, it was the ideal gift for a nobleman to present to a royal or other prominent person—as a wedding gift, perhaps, or in expectation of or in gratitude for a favour. The lavish use of ultramarine, the most expensive of the pigments used by artists, and especially gold leaf, indicates that the book was intended for someone important.

All manuscripts were made in much the same way. The illuminator worked on parchment made from the skins of calves (vellum), sheep and goats. (For the best-quality manuscripts, the parchment was stained purple with a shellfish dye, or green with a verdigris dye.) First he would draw the outline of the design using a quill pen dipped in ink made from lampblack. Next he would treat the areas to be gilded with an adhesive such as stag's horn glue. The gold was applied in leaves beaten to the thinness of a cobweb, and was then burnished (polished with an animal's tooth) to give it a smooth, reflecting surface. Some of the most common pigments used in manuscript illuminations were malachite for green, vermilion (made from red lead) or the less expensive cinnabar for red, and saffron for yellow; other yellows and browns were made from different-coloured earths. The pigments were bound in beaten or filtered egg white, known as glair, and it is this that gives the colours their fresh appearance. Depth of colour was sometimes thought to be increased by adding honey to the glair.

Sewing shown in writing: a manuscript illumination depicting the
Virgin Mary at her needlepoint.

Writing shown on sewing: a section of the Bayeux Tapestry commemorating Edward receiving Harold at Westminster.

The text was written, or rather copied, by a scribe, who left spaces for the pictures, initial letters and borders to be filled in by the illuminator. Some of the most delicate painting is found in the ornamental margins, which incorporate elements that may or may not be relevant to the text. Herbals, describing and illustrating plants and their characteristics and medicinal properties, were the source for some of these miscellaneous details, as were bestiaries, which catalogued animals real and fabled. Further inspiration came from the work done in other crafts.

Birds and beasts, fish, insects and flowers appear in exquisite detail in medieval illuminated manuscripts, and they appear, too, in stained glass and tapestries. Scrolling and foliate forms, grotesques and the geometric and repeating patterns found in the border decorations relate to the motifs and designs of contemporary metalwork, architectural stonecarving, the wood-carving of ecclesiastical furniture and misericords, and needlework.

The relationship between the arts of manuscript illumination and needle-work is particularly close where painters were involved in the design, as in the ecclesiastical embroidery known as Opus Anglicanum, which was produced in England in the years between 900 and 1500 and much admired on the Continent. The embroidery was done on linen or velvet cloth in coloured silks, gold and silver thread, pearls and occasionally jewels (canvas was not used until much later). The gold on medieval copes, laid on the surface and fastened from the back with linen thread, would have gleamed like the gold on contemporary manuscripts. Some of the same figures and narrative scenes found in book paintings are depicted in embroidery, framed by the same quatrefoil forms and Gothic tracery; and sometimes strong similarities can be seen between the style characteristic of a school of illuminators and particular pieces of embroidery.

The Bayeux Tapestry, for instance, is thought to have been designed and drawn by members of the Canterbury school of manuscript painters. In the tapestry's seventy-nine scenes all the ephemera of contemporary life are represented—tables and seats, needlework cushions and curtains, the clothes worn by kings, ecclesiastics and soldiers, regalia and weaponry—along with many of the incidental details that appear in the illuminations of Psalters and Books of Hours. In the border, the same range of real and imaginary animals is depicted, and various of the rustic pursuits illustrated in medieval calendars.

The embroidery of the Bayeux Tapestry was carried out in eight different shades of wool. The dyeing of raw materials and cloth, and the cultivation of plants such as madder, for red, and woad, for blue, was important and well-rewarded work in the Middle Ages. Dyeing was done commercially in towns, where red brazilwood, kermes (obtained from an insect found in the Mediterranean and Near East) and other imported dyes might be used. In rural areas all manner of local plants, wood barks and fruits were put into the cauldron to colour textiles.

Silk rather than wool thread was used for the finest needlework, such as Opus Anglicanum. Copes, orphreys, altar frontals and palls were embroidered by nuns in convents and by the female lay communities of Beguines, who lived by the labour of their hands. The nuns also made secular embroideries, such as belts, and purses for Books of Hours and other valued possessions, as gifts for visitors. In England in the fourteenth century the nuns had become so absorbed in their silk embroidery that they had to be warned officially against neglecting their religious duties.

Both men and women were employed in the embroidery workshops in towns, where they were subject to guild regulations as in any other medieval craft, and also in the workshops of royal and noble households. On the whole, however, needlework was women's work. Spinning wool and the flax for linen cloth and thread was considered a female occupation, practised by women from all ranks of society. The lady of the house would involve herself in the production of everyday clothes, tablecloths, sheets and pillowcases, worked in linen on linen.

Tabards, the surcoats that knights wore over their armour, and the scarves worn on top, the hoods, sleeves, mantles, bracelets, pennants, banners and other chivalric paraphernalia demanded all the skills of ladies' needles.

> *'It will increase their peace, enlarge their store,*
> *To use their tongues less, and their needles more.'*

> The Needle's Excellency, JOHN TAYLER

Pair of Hunting Cushions

Inspired by the Book of Hours of the Duchess of Burgundy

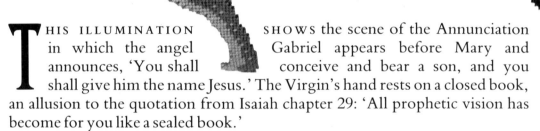

THIS ILLUMINATION in which the angel announces, 'You shall shall give him the name Jesus.' The Virgin's hand rests on a closed book, an allusion to the quotation from Isaiah chapter 29: 'All prophetic vision has become for you like a sealed book.'

SHOWS the scene of the Annunciation Gabriel appears before Mary and conceive and bear a son, and you

The court of the Dukes of Burgundy during the fifteenth century was powerful and wealthy and the elaborate gold-embroidered dress worn by the Virgin Mary is very much a reflection of how the Duchess of Burgundy, owner of this book, would have dressed. Behind her are ranged the seraphim and cherubim, easily distinguished by the colour of their wings (red for seraphim, blue for cherubim). Through the church door and windows can be seen an unusual night-time townscape, the brilliance of the expensive lamp-light and candlepower indicating that, once again, we are in a wealthy Burgundian town.

The sense of receding perspective is accentuated by the architectural frame through which the event is seen. The border has a typically medieval exuberance: a huntsman blows his horn and his two dogs leap forward into a thicket of pinks, columbine (one of eight herbs used against the plague), thistles, violets and peaflowers, while the deer races off the other side of the page. The rather unattractive snail and beetle are thrown into the mêlée, unconcerned by their relative enormity; the painter is clearly trying to convey the rich diversity of God's kingdom.

An illumination of the Annunciation, taken from the Book of Hours produced for the Duchess of Burgundy c.1450.

ERE IS ANOTHER ILLUMINATED MANUSCRIPT which provides one with almost too much material from which to choose. For me, however, the story of the chase which is being told along the bottom of the page stands out more than any other design in the book.

I could not help but be drawn by the almost surreal mixture of reality and fantasy: the greyhounds are so life-like that they could have just leapt off a modern race track, whilst a threatening-looking dragonfly has been painted virtually the same size (so odd did it look, being so out of scale, that you will find it is missing from the stitching design); the hunter and deer, accurate in every detail, are surrounded by oversized foliage and ornamental scrolls, providing even more contrast. With the addition of a shower of gold spots—worked in cotton on the cushion for a gilded effect—no part of the vellum is left undecorated.

The two cushion designs could be combined and stitched as one, to form one large rectangular cushion, or worked as they are and then framed.

'I had no sooner my hounds let go,/But the hart was overthrow./
Then every man began to blow,/With "Trororo! Trororo!
Trororo! Trow!"/We shall have game and sport full now.'
Stag-Hunt, ANON.

DEER CUSHION CHART

MATERIALS:

DMC wool and stranded cotton skeins as listed in colour key (23 colours)
   Use 1 whole strand of wool/12 strands of cotton per stitching thread

12-count antique deluxe canvas
   Design size: 18.5 x 13.5in (46.5 x 34cm)
   Canvas size: 22 x 18in (55 x 45cm)

Backing fabric: 22 x 18in (55 x 45cm)
Braid: 1.8yds (1.65m)
Feather pad: 18 x 14in (45 x 35cm)

See page 122 for making-up instructions

KEY TO COLOURS *(showing DMC brand number, general colour name and number of skeins required)*:

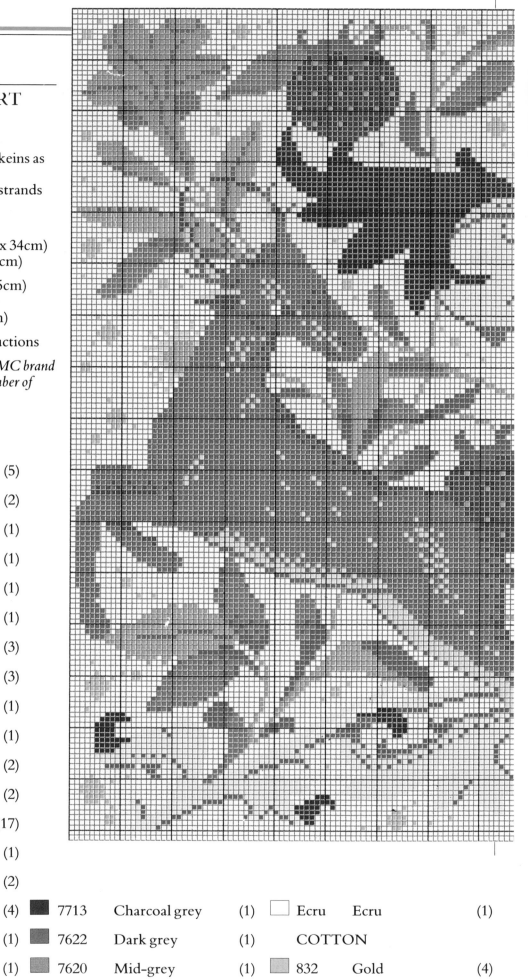

WOOLS

	7472	Yellow	(5)
	7457	Copper	(2)
	7920	Red	(1)
	7127	Dark red	(1)
	7950	Dusty pink	(1)
	7202	Pink	(1)
	7318	Royal blue	(3)
	7307	Navy blue	(3)
	7323	Grey-blue	(1)
	7306	Light blue	(1)
	7370	Light green	(2)
	7540	Dark green	(2)
	7510	Light beige	(17)
	7511	Mid-beige	(1)
	7833	Dark gold	(2)
	7525	Mid-brown	(4)
	7527	Dark brown	(1)
	Noir	Black	(1)

7713	Charcoal grey	(1)
7622	Dark grey	(1)
7620	Mid-grey	(1)

Ecru	Ecru	(1)

COTTON

832	Gold	(4)

HUNTING HOUNDS CUSHION CHART

MATERIALS:

DMC wool and stranded cotton skeins as listed in colour key (20 colours)
Use 1 whole strand of wool/12 strands of cotton per stitching thread

12-count antique deluxe canvas
Design size: 18.5 x 13.5in
(46.5 x 34cm)
Canvas size: 22 x 18in (55 x 45cm)

Backing fabric: 22 x 18in (55 x 45cm)
Braid: 1.8yds (1.65m)
Feather pad: 18 x 14in (45 x 35cm)

See page 122 for making-up instructions

KEY TO COLOURS *(showing DMC brand number, general colour name and number of skeins required):*

WOOLS

	7472	Yellow	(5)
	7833	Dark gold	(2)
	7457	Copper	(2)
	7920	Red	(1)
	7127	Dark red	(1)
	7491	Flesh	(1)
	7200	Light pink	(1)
	7202	Mid-pink	(1)
	7318	Royal blue	(5)
	7307	Navy blue	(2)
	7370	Light green	(2)
	7540	Dark green	(2)
	7510	Light beige	(20)
	7525	Mid-brown	(1)
	Noir	Black	(1)
	7275	Dark grey	(2)
	7713	Charcoal grey	(1)

	7323	Mid-grey	(1)
	7321	Light grey	(3)

COTTON

	832	Gold	(4)

Oak-leaf Footstool

Inspired by the Livre des Merveilles

THE SURVIVAL OF the glorious fresh greens, pinks and vermilion in this manuscript and the delicacy with which it is painted is a testimony to its creator, the Boucicault Master. As so often, the name of this great master of the miniaturist's art is not known, and he is called after his most famous work, in this case an elaborate Book of Hours made for the Maréchal de Boucicault. He was born in Bruges but did his greatest illuminations in Paris in the early fifteenth century. In addition to his outstanding colouring, the Boucicault Master is renowned for his effects of light and perspective, as exemplified by this detailed interior with its fireplace and open stained-glass windows.

This manuscript, the *Livre des Merveilles*, gives an account of the wondrous sights seen during the Eastern travels of Marco Polo and other travellers of the thirteenth and fourteenth centuries. It was compiled by the English monk, John Hayton, who is shown presenting the book to John the Fearless, Duke of Burgundy. The creation of such extensively ornamented and illustrated manuscripts was a costly and prestigious undertaking, so that the originator or patron of the scheme frequently had his own portrait painted as a frontispiece. Here the Duke sits in splendour and further allusions are made to him in the heraldic devices at each corner of the page, his connection to the French royal family signified by the cloth scattered with fleurs-de-lis over his chair and the fleurs-de-lis emblazoned on the decorated initial letter. Hopefully, he had time to enjoy the manuscript before he was killed in 1419.

John Hayton presents a copy of his book to John the Fearless, Duke of Burgundy, from the Livre des Merveilles *produced in the early fifteenth century.*

Cy commence le liure frere Jehan hayton de lordre de pre monstre touse ...
gernam du roy darmenie qui parle des merueilles des xiiij roiaul mes daise.
Le royaume de cattay est tenu pour le plus noble roy
aume et le plus riche qui sont ou monde et est sur le riua
ge de la mer oceane. Tantes istes ya de mer que len nen
puet pas bien sauoir le nombre. Les gens qui habitt
en cellui royaume sont appelles cathains. et se treuuet
entre eube mains beaux homnes et femmes selonc
leur nacion. mais tous ont les yeulx moult petis. et ont pou de barbe. Celles
gens ont lettres qui de beaute ressamblent a lettres latines. et parlent une
langaige qui moult est duuerse des autres langues du monde. La creance de
ceste gent est moult duuerse. Car aucuns croient au soulcil. autres a la lu

THE VIBRANT RUSTS AND GREENS of this manuscript jumped out of the
page at me the first time I saw it—so much so that I knew straight away that
it would be in the final selection of designs. I would have loved to use the
entire page but for practical purposes I had to limit myself to the centre section
of the bottom border, leaving the lion and the eagle behind.

With fairly simple designs like this which have a single colour background
it is easy to experiment with different colourways. I think the leaf motif would
also look stunning set against a dark background such as chocolate or
midnight blue; a stool base in very dark wood could then be used to set off the
colours to best effect.

Rectangular shapes such as this may be put to alternative uses, as bolster-
type cushions, for example, or set as a centre panel on a larger cushion made
from another fabric.

*'Summer is icumen in,/Loudly sing, cuckoo!/Groweth seed and
bloweth mead/and springeth the wood anew.'* ANON.

OAK-LEAF FOOTSTOOL CHART

MATERIALS:

DMC wool skeins as listed in colour key (12 colours)
   Use 1 whole strand of wool per stitching thread

10-count antique deluxe canvas
   Design size: 23 x 10in
   (57.5 x 25cm)
   Canvas size: 27 x 14in
   (67.5 x 35cm)

Footstool pad and base (see page 128 for suppliers)

See page 124 for making-up instructions

KEY TO COLOURS *(showing DMC brand number, general colour name and number of skeins required):*

▨	7947	Orange	(5)
▨	7360	Rust	(3)
■	7303	Dark rust	(2)
▨	7171	Light peach	(1)
▨	7144	Salmon	(2)
▨	7799	Light blue	(1)
□	7579	Light yellow	(12)

	7798	Mid-blue	(1)
	7820	Dark blue	(1)
	7548	Light green	(2)
	7547	Mid-green	(5)
	7367	Dark green	(3)

Fleur-de-lis Pencil Box

Inspired by a French Book of Hours

CHARACTERISTIC OF this border combines terns. The fleur-de-lis is a heraldic lozenge, but the of infilling the fleurs-de-lis with he has decorated with abstract leafy scrolls.

MEDIEVAL ORNAMENT, naturalism with abstract patterns. the dominant form, set within artist has had the unusual conceit daisy sprigs. The rest of the panel

The fleur-de-lis, a stylized lily which had long been recognized as a symbol of purity, came to represent the Virgin Mary. According to legend, the Merovingian king, Clovis, chose the flower as his emblem when he converted to Christianity in the fifth century; it was later adopted by the French royal family from the twelfth century onwards, until its use was forbidden during the Revolution.

This page, seen in detail, clearly shows the illuminator's use of the two most important—and expensive—colours used in miniature painting: gold and blue. The gold had to be pure gold leaf, which would not tarnish, and was finely burnished on to the vellum page. The blue, ultramarine, could only be produced from powdered lapis lazuli, a semi-precious stone found, at that time, principally in Persia.

A detail of fleurs-de-lis, taken from an illumination in a French Book of Hours produced c.1500.

ad adiuuandū

loria patri

uait erīt. a

ector poten

ut ē f. lxb

efeat ⁊ salut

n eternu dno

Quomodo dile

uterna pdi

nquos odio

ea indiaum

⁊. Sancti vero do

toribus traditi ad

nalia ducti sunt.

I ALWAYS FIND fleur-de-lis motifs attractive, and this one almost shimmers with its use of precious pigments. It is a perfect example of the medieval artist's technique. While to our eye, so used to seeing images automatically flipped or mirrored using modern graphic techniques, the illumination appears to be an exact repeat of the fleur-de-lis shape, it was actually copied using nothing more than the artist's skills of eye and hand. Tracing paper let alone computer graphics would not be available for centuries; I was very relieved to be able to use both.

Here worked in cotton on a very small scale, this design could be used for virtually any other type of project by increasing the size of the canvas and working in wool.

'Maiden in the moor lay,/In the moor lay/Seven nights full and a day./. . . Well was her bower/What was her bower?/The red rose and the lily-flower.' The Maid of the Moor, ANON.

FLEURS-DE-LIS PENCIL BOX CHART

MATERIALS:

DMC stranded cotton skeins as listed in colour key (11 colours)
   Use 6 strands of cotton per stitching thread

18-count antique deluxe canvas
   Design size: 4 x 11.5in
   (10 x 29cm)
   Canvas size: 7 x 14in
   (17.5 x 35cm)

Pencil-box pad and base (see page 128 for suppliers)

See page 124 for making-up instructions

KEY TO COLOURS *(showing DMC brand number, general colour name and number of skeins required):*

☐	677	Light yellow	(4)
	676	Gold	(1)
	816	Dark red	(1)
	760	Pink	(1)
	797	Light blue	(2)
	820	Dark blue	(4)
	3052	Light green	(1)
	501	Dark green	(1)
	434	Brown	(1)
☐	762	Light grey	(5)
☐	Blanc	White	(1)

Florentine Curtain Pelmet and Tie-backs

Inspired by the Dialogues of Plato

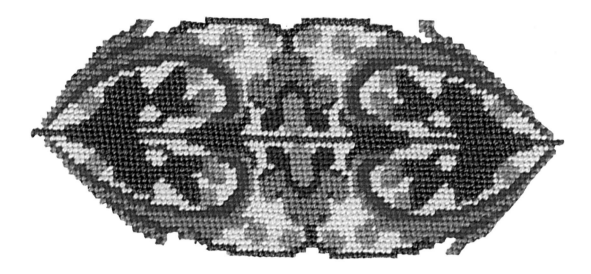

T HIS MANUSCRIPT, an Italian Renaissance edition of the *Dialogues* of Plato translated into Latin from the original Greek by Ficino, was made for Lorenzo di Medici. The whole Medici family were famous for their patronage of the arts and learning, and *c.* 1524 Lorenzo, known as 'the Magnificent', commissioned Michelangelo to design a library, the Biblioteca Laurenziana, in Florence. This magnificent building was intended to house the large collection of manuscripts that had been accumulated by himself and his father, Cosimo, and this version of the *Dialogues* can still be found there today.

Supported by angels, the coat of arms of the ruling Florentine Medici family is emblazoned at the bottom of the page. One of the balls has been adorned with fleurs-de-lis, the symbol of Florence.

In comparison to the earlier French and Flemish Gothic manuscripts, this one is of a much more sophisticated design. The decoration is carefully confined to the borders of the page and consists only of elegant and subtly coloured scrolling foliage, with no superfluous ornamental flourishes or grotesques.

The script is no longer Gothic, but minuscule, a much looser and more legible hand based on earlier Romanesque lettering and the precursor of italic handwriting.

The preface to a copy of the Dialogues of Plato *translated into Latin by Ficino, made for Lorenzo di Medici in the early sixteenth century.*

omia suauiterq̃ disponens Magnanime Laurenti statuit
religionē sanctam non solvm ṗphetis et sibyllis sacrisq̃ arma
re doctoribus: verx et pia quadam eleganti q̃ philosophia singu
lariter exornare. vt ipa pietas omnium origo bonōr tā secu
ra tandē inter omis sapientiæ & eloquentiæ ṗfessores incedēt
q̃ tuta inter domesticos conquiescit. Oportebat. x. religione.
quæ vnica est ad felicitatē via non rudioribus tm hominibus vere etiam peritio
ribus comunem fore. qua qdem duce omis ad beatitudinē cuius gra nati sumus; et
ad quam consequendam comuni stvdio laboramvs: facilius tuti q̃ puenire possem?
Itaq̃ deus omnipotēs statutis teporibus diuinu Platonis animu ab alto demisit: vita
ingenio eloquo q̃ mirabili religione sacram apd omis gentes illustratvrv̄. Cvm vo
ad hæc vsq̃ secula sol platonicvs non dum palam latinis gentibus oriret. Cosm?
Italiæ decvs et insignis pietate vir platonicam lucem religioni admodvm salutarē
a Græcis ad Latinos propagare contendens me potissimvm intra suos lares plu
rimvm educatvm tanto operi destinauit. Ego aut etsi a tenera ætate nominis
platonici cvltor: rē tn adeo grauem non meis qdem sed alti tvi Cosmi ṗperis au
spicijs svm aggressvs: sperans diuinam opem tam necessario tamq̃ pio officio non
defutvram. Hac ergo iprimis spe ductvs Academiam svm ingressus: decemq̃ ex
ea Platonis nostri dialogos Cosmo, prius q̃ natune concederet Latinos feci. Post ei
obitvm patri tuo Petro prestantissime viro dialogos nouem legendos dedi. Postq̃ vo
Petrvs e vita decessit: Fortuna præclaris sepe operibus inuida inuitvm me a tradue
tionis officio distrahebat. Verx tv ex religionis cvltor et phiæ patronvs me ad
inceptvm omni fauore et auxilio reuocasti. Quaobre ad institutvm munvs feli
cibus itervm auspicijs svm regressvs. Neq̃ traduxi tantvm: verx et ṗtim argu
mentis mentem ṗstrinxa platonicam: ṗtim quoad potui breuibus comentarijs expli
caui. Opus itaq̃ totv̄ diuino auxilio iam absolutvm tibi libentissime dedico? Ad
quem illa etiam quæ maioribus tuis inscripta sunt iure hereditario ṗtinent: vi
rvm ṗfecto auitæ paternæq̃ inpatria colenda virtutis herede. Leges aut in
ter dialogos funebrem Platonis orationem pio fratri tuo Iuliano dicatum. Prete
rea vbi ad librvm de regno perueneris: videbis Federicvm vrbinatem ducem
eo die à me honoratvm: quo ipe tuas ædes honorifice salutauit. Non solvm vo
septe atq̃ triginta libri qui solo tvo insigniti sunt titulo: sed cuncti denuq̃ tui
sunt: onqdem omis tui gratia sunt absoluti: atq̃ ego svm tuus. Neq̃ vo me
platonicvm in his libris stilvm omnino expressisse profiteor: Neq̃ rurs? abullo
quis admodvm doctiore vnq̃ exprimi posse confido: stily inq̃ no tam humano
eloquio q̃ diuino oraculo simile: sæpe quidē tonantē alti?: sæpe vo nectarea
suauitate manantē: semper aut archana cælestia cōplectentē. Profecto que

'Plainly, I cannot praise;/Ye be, as I devine,/The pretty primrose,/The goodly columbine./With marjoram gentle,/The flower of goodlihead,/Embroidered the mantle/Is of your maidenhead.' To Mistress Margery Wentworth,
JOHN SKELTON

THE COLOURING AND STYLE of this manuscript is typically Florentine, and you can still find decorated boxes, desk accessories and gifts which use this style on sale in Florence today.

Worked in pretty pinks and blues it makes an ideal bedroom set. Besides using them as curtain accessories, the pelmet would make a stylish feature mounted on the wall above a bed, whilst the tie-back design could be used to create little decorative cushions for the bed. The chubby angels could even be interpreted as cupids if the needlepoint was intended as a wedding gift, and the central lozenge adapted to contain the names of the couple and the date of their marriage.

Experiment with different colourways to complement your décor: bold contrasting colours on a dramatic dark-toned background or more subtle, barely-there shades on the palest grey or beige background.

Worked in cottons on a smaller gauge canvas, the pelmet design could be shortened to make an attractive if chunky book mark, or, lengthened and with the addition of a buckle, a stylish belt. Used vertically, the end section is also an ideal shape for use as a bell-pull.

'Here is lily of largesse,/Here is periwinkle of prowess,/Here is sunflower of sweetness/and queen of faithfulness.' Blow,
Northern Wind, ANON.

FLORENTINE CURTAIN TIE-BACK CHART

MATERIALS:

Paterna stranded Persian yarn skeins
as listed in colour key (9 colours)
   Use 2 strands per stitching thread

12-count white deluxe canvas
   Design size: 20.5 x 7.5in
   (51.5 x 19cm)
   Canvas size: 25 x 12in
   (62.5 x 30cm)

Backing fabric: 25 x 12in
   (62.5 x 30cm)
Braid: approx. 1.8yds (1.65m) per
   tie-back

See page 125 for making-up
instructions

KEY TO COLOURS *(showing
Paterna brand number, general colour
name and number of skeins required):*

☐	263	Cream	(20)
☐	734	Light gold	(6)
☐	732	Dark gold	(2)
☐	955	Light pink	(5)
☐	952	Dark pink	(2)
☐	653	Light blue	(4)
☐	560	Dark blue	(3)
☐	522	Mid-green	(6)
☐	602	Dark green	(1)

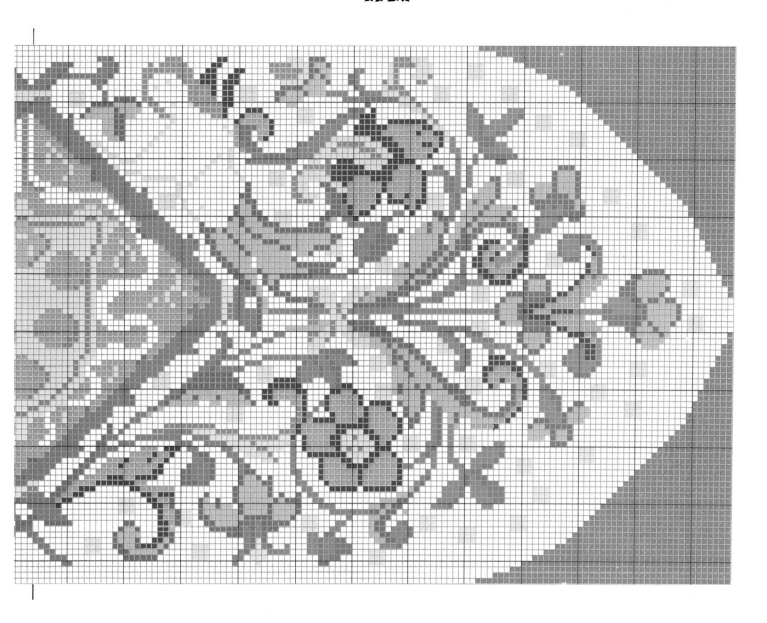

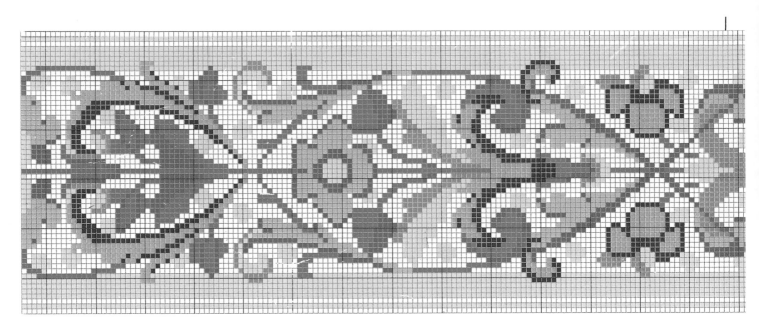

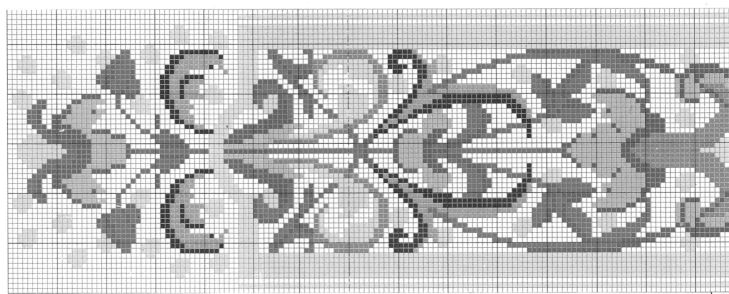

FLORENTINE CURTAIN PELMET CHART

MATERIALS:

Paterna stranded Persian yarn skeins as listed in colour key (9 colours)
    Use 1 complete thread (3 strands) per stitching thread

10-count white deluxe canvas
    Design size: 57 x 6in
    (142.5 x 15cm)
    Canvas size: 61 x 10in
    (152.5 x 25cm)

Backing fabric: 61 x 10in
    (152.5 x 25cm)

Heavy-duty velcro

See page 125 for making-up instructions

KEY TO COLOURS *(showing Paterna brand number, general colour name and number of skeins required)*:

	Number	Colour	Skeins
	263	Cream	(18)
	734	Light gold	(15)
	732	Dark gold	(3)
	955	Light pink	(4)
	952	Dark pink	(4)
	653	Light blue	(4)
	560	Dark blue	(4)
	522	Mid-green	(6)
	602	Dark green	(4)

Iris Bell-pull

Inspired by the Hastings Book of Hours

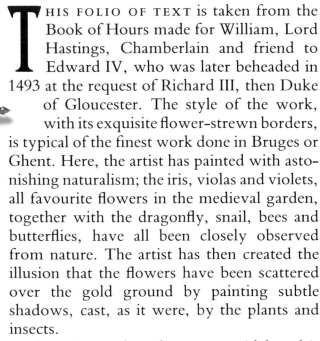

THIS FOLIO OF TEXT is taken from the Book of Hours made for William, Lord Hastings, Chamberlain and friend to Edward IV, who was later beheaded in 1493 at the request of Richard III, then Duke of Gloucester. The style of the work, with its exquisite flower-strewn borders, is typical of the finest work done in Bruges or Ghent. Here, the artist has painted with astonishing naturalism; the iris, violas and violets, all favourite flowers in the medieval garden, together with the dragonfly, snail, bees and butterflies, have all been closely observed from nature. The artist has then created the illusion that the flowers have been scattered over the gold ground by painting subtle shadows, cast, as it were, by the plants and insects.

Blue irises such as these were widely cultivated all over Europe. As with so many popular medieval flowers, they were grown not only for their beauty and scent, but also for their more practical uses: the dried leaves were used to stuff chair seats; the sweet-smelling powdered root (called orris) was widely used as an air freshener; and the juice formed the basis of a green dye used in the production of textiles. For this fifteenth-century artist, the iris would also have signified the Virgin Mary, and on the opposite page of the manuscript he has depicted her on the Flight into Egypt.

'Of lily, of rose and of iris,
  Of primrose and of fleur-de-lis,
Of all the flowers, at my devise,
  That flower of Jesus yet bears the prize.'

The Fairest Flower, JOHN AUDELAY

RIGHT: *An illumination of the Flight into Egypt, taken from the* Hastings Book of Hours, *made for William, Lord Hastings, c.1480.*

D eus in ad
iutorium
meum in
tende. Do
mine ad
adiuuandum me festina.
Gloria patri et filio et spi
ritu sancto Sicut erat in
prinapio et nunc et semper
et in seaula seculorum amen
Post partum. An
Letatus sum in hus que
dicta sunt michi in domi
domini ibimus Stantes
erant pedes nostri in atriis

THIS DESIGN FEATURES FLOWERS and insects painted with the kind of super-realism that the medieval artist brought to specimens studied in close detail. One can imagine them laid on a piece of vellum in front of him; by copying from life and including the shadows cast on the page, he could create an almost three-dimensional effect.

To keep the design in proportion, I was able to use only one part of the page. The shape would also make an attractive pen- or jewellery-box lid. Alternatively, worked in wools on a larger canvas, it could form the centre panel of a fabric cushion. For details of how to hang the bell-pull see page 125.

'The busy bee her honey now rememb's;/Winter is worn that was the flowers' bale.' Spring, HENRY HOWARD

IRIS BELL-PULL CHART

MATERIALS:

DMC stranded cotton skeins as listed in colour key (19 colours)
  Use 12 strands of cotton per stitching thread

12-count antique deluxe canvas
  Design size: 5 x 18in (12.5 x 45cm)
  Canvas size: 9 x 22in (22.5 x 55cm)

Backing fabric: 9 x 22in (22.5 x 55cm)
Braid: 1.5yds (1.35m)
Rod: 7in (17.5cm)

See page 125 for making-up instructions

KEY TO COLOURS *(showing DMC brand number, general colour name and number of skeins required):*

	3047	Light yellow	(1)
	727	Mid-yellow	(1)
	3046	Gold	(11)
	3045	Dark yellow	(1)
	832	Dark gold	(2)
	3033	Light biscuit	(1)
	794	Light blue	(2)
	793	Mid-blue	(1)
	791	Dark blue	(1)
	988	Green	(1)
	3022	Grey-green	(1)
	613	Dark biscuit	(2)
	645	Dark grey-brown	(1)
	Noir	Black	(1)
	413	Gunmetal	(1)
	647	Mid-grey	(1)
	415	Light grey	(1)
	762	Very light grey	(2)
	Blanc	White	(1)

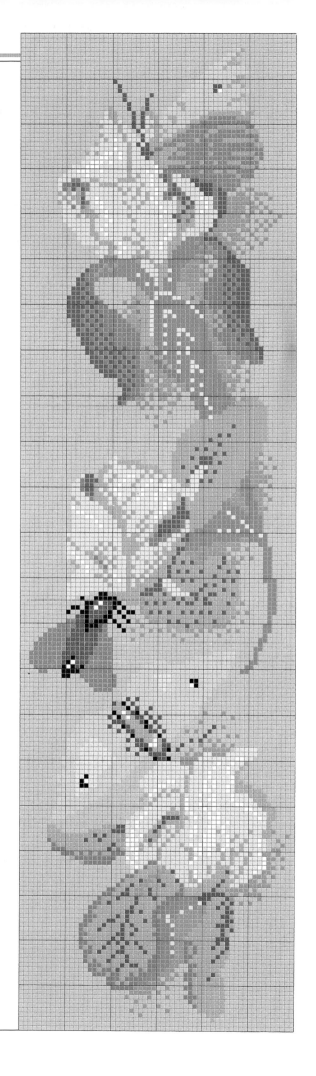

Heart-shaped Herb Cushion

Inspired by the Hours of Le Camus

'Y OU RELEASE MY LIPS, Lord, and my mouth sings out your praise.' So says the text accompanying this scene of the Pentecost, or Descent of the Holy Ghost, marking the birth of the Church.

The Virgin Mary and the apostles are gathered together on the Jewish feast of Pentecost, having returned to Jerusalem after witnessing the Ascension of Christ. The Holy Spirit is represented by a dove, and from this radiate beams of light and tongues of flame. The Bible describes the 'tongues like flames of fire, dispersed among them and resting on each one. And they were all filled with the Holy Spirit and began to talk in other tongues, as the Spirit gave them power of utterance.'

The hearts in the border, from which this project was developed, could be seen as symbols of sacred as well as profane love. What seems so incongruous to modern eyes, but clearly not to the artist and owner of this manuscript, is the inclusion of the grotesque griffin-like and monkey figures among the blue and gold arabesques.

In medieval Christian inconography the monkey or ape represented the devil and its presence here is in precisely the same vein as the figures found on roof bosses, gargoyles and carved capitals of the great European Gothic cathedrals and churches. The source of many of these bizarre hybrid animals was the *Liber Physiologus*, a bestiary or catalogue of animals real and imagined, the descriptions of which were an inspiration to the medieval craftsman, painter, stonemason and woodcarver.

An illumination of the Pentecost, taken from the Hours of Le Camus, *produced in the mid-fifteenth century.*

Omine labia mea
aperies. Et os
meum anuciabit
laudem tuam.

*'My maiden Isabel,/Reflaring rosabel/. . . The sovereign
rosemary,/The pretty strawberry.'* To Mistress Isabel Pennel,
JOHN SKELTON.

ALTHOUGH JUST A SMALL DEVICE on the entire page this heart-shaped
design makes a very strong statement on its own, the blood red of the
flowers contrasting well with the neutral background.

Used for containing sweet-smelling herbs or pot-pourri this is a truly
medieval project since such solutions were the only antidote to foul smells at
that time. Today it may be used as a fragrant addition to wardrobes, chests of
drawers or as a green alternative to synthetic room fresheners. Braid made
from the cotton thread used for stitching has been used to trim the heart. It
also provides a means of hanging the sachet, although ribbon could be used.

Worked slightly larger, this shape would make attractive bedroom
cushions and could be worked in pastel shades of cotton or wool for a softer
colourway, depending on your décor.

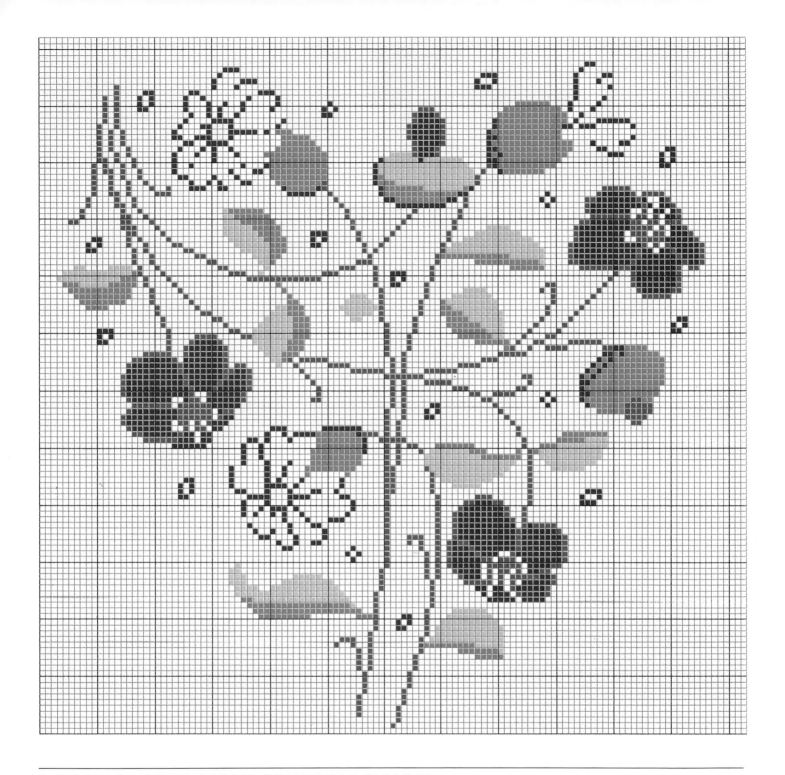

HEART-SHAPED HERB CUSHION CHART

MATERIALS:

DMC stranded cotton skeins as listed in colour key (7 colours)
Use 6 strands of cotton per stitching thread

18-count antique deluxe canvas
Design size: 7.5 x 6.5in
(19 x 16.5cm)
Canvas size: 11x10in (27.5x25cm)

Backing fabric: 11x10in (27.5x25cm)
Stuffing

Extra cotton to make braid
(see page 124)

See page 123 for making-up instructions

KEY TO COLOURS *(showing DMC brand number, general colour name and number of skeins required):*

	3047	Light yellow	(8)
	349	Light red	(1)
	993	Light green	(1)
	991	Dark green	(1)
	355	Dark red	(1)
	3031	Dark brown	(1)
	Blanc	White	(1)

Four Floral Chair Seat Covers and Rug

Inspired by the Playfair Book of Hours

A RICHLY DECORATED PAGE from a French Book of Hours of the late fifteenth century was the inspiration for this project. The central panel depicts the four Evangelists, the authors of the four New Testament Gospels. Each saint would have been readily identifiable by the symbolic figure beside him: St John by an eagle; St Matthew by a man; St Mark by a lion; and St Luke by an ox. St John the Baptist is recognizable in the smaller niche by the lamb that he holds, a symbol of Christ on the Cross. Under the Roman Emperor Domitian, many early Christians were persecuted, and at the bottom of the page St John the Evangelist is shown having to endure immersion in a barrel of boiling oil.

Books of Hours, used as personal devotional books, were manufactured in huge numbers during the Middle Ages; they were considered a necessity by all families from the bourgeois class upwards, and were often presented to new couples as a wedding present. Made of vellum, they combined the skills of the scribe, who wrote out the text, and the artist, who decorated the page with illuminations, borders and elaborate initial letters.

The core of the book was always the Hours of the Virgin, prayers and psalms in honour of the Virgin Mary which the devout were expected to recite at each of the canonical hours of the day: Matins, Lauds, Prime, Terce, Sext, None, Vespers and Compline. In addition, there was a calendar with the saints' days and feast days accentuated in gold, blue or red (hence 'red letter days'), and a sequence of the Gospels, Hours of the Cross and Hours of the Holy Spirit, along with penitential psalms, litany, office of the dead and suffrages of the saints.

An illumination of the Four Evangelists, taken from the Playfair Book of Hours, *produced in the late fifteenth century.*

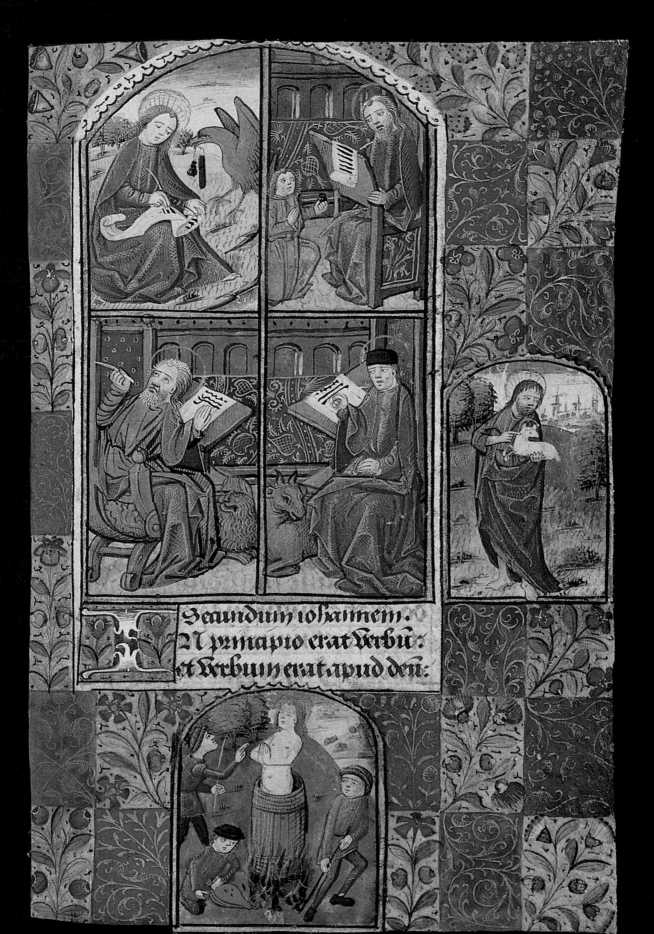

Secundum iohannem.
In principio erat verbū:
et verbum erat apud deū:

DEPENDING ON THE NUMBER of chairs that you have, the designs may be used in any permutation to create a set. Besides using the pads on the seats of the chairs, they may also be tied to the backs as cushions.

The two-tone design uses rich red or blue wool for the background and gold cotton for the 'gilding'. A matching gold braid has been used to finish all the cushions and tag ends, or tassels made from the cotton thread used for stitching, have then been added to the ends (see pages 122–3).

The same panels have been sewn together to create a rug which exactly recreates the layout from the original manuscript (see page 126).

'Of a rose, a lovely rose,/Of a rose is all my song./Listeneth, sirs, both old and young/How this rose began to spring;/ A rose so much to my liking/ In all this world I know not one.' Of a Rose, a Lovely Rose, ANON.

'The silver is white, red is the gold;/The robes they lay in fold./. . . And through the glass window shines the sun./ How should I love and I so young?/The bailey beareth the bell away;/the lily, the rose, the rose I lay.' The Bridal Morn, ANON.

'The columbine, the mint,/The lily-flower well set,/The proper violet.' To Mistress Isabel Pennell, JOHN SKELTON

RED FLORAL CHAIR SEAT COVER CHART

MATERIALS:

DMC wool skeins as listed in colour key
(6 colours)
    Use 1 whole strand of wool per stitching
thread

10-count antique deluxe canvas
    Design size: 14.5 x 12in (36.5 x 30cm)
    Canvas size: 19 x 16in (47.5 x 40cm)

Backing fabric: 19 x 16in (47.5 x 40cm)
Chair seat pad: 14.5 x 12 x 1.5in
    (36.5 x 30 x 4cm) foam
Braid: 3.5yds (3.15m), allowing a little
    extra if loops are needed for tassels
Tassels/tag ends: 4 (see page 122–3)

See page 122 for making-up instructions

KEY TO COLOURS *(showing DMC brand
number, general colour name and number of
skeins required):*

■	7108	Red	(3)
□	7853	Pink	(1)
▨	7424	Light green	(3)
▨	7428	Dark green	(3)
□	7724	Beige	(13)
■	7535	Dark brown	(2)

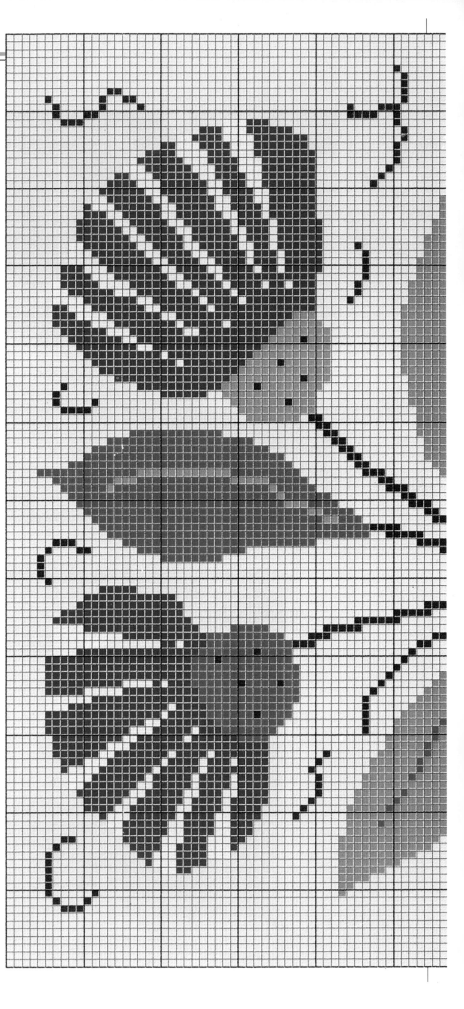

BLUE FLORAL CHAIR SEAT COVER CHART

MATERIALS:

DMC wool skeins as listed in colour key
(7 colours)
    Use 1 whole strand of wool per stitching
thread

10-count antique deluxe canvas
    Design size: 14.5 x 12in (36.5 x 30cm)
    Canvas size: 19 x 16in (47.5 x 40cm)

Backing fabric: 19 x 16in (47.5 x 40cm)
Chair seat pad: 14.5 x 12 x 1.5in
    (36.5 x 30 x 4cm) foam
Braid: 3.5yds (3.15m), allowing a little
    extra if loops are needed for tassels
Tassels/tag ends: 4 (see page 122–3)

See page 122 for making-up instructions

KEY TO COLOURS (*showing DMC brand
number, general colour name and number of
skeins required*):

■	7108	Red	(1)
■	7319	Dark blue	(4)
■	7424	Light green	(2)
■	7428	Dark green	(3)
□	7724	Beige	(12)
■	7535	Brown	(1)
□	Blanc	White	(1)

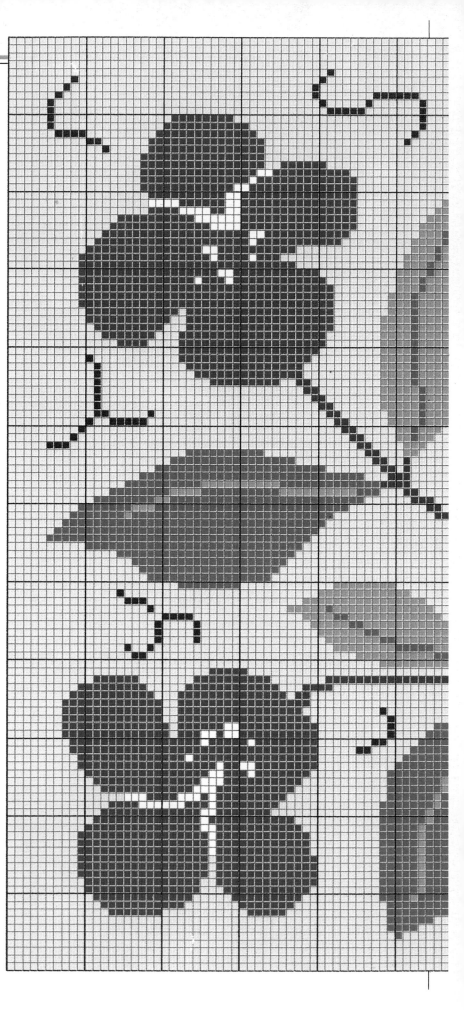

WHITE FLORAL CHAIR
SEAT COVER CHART

MATERIALS:

DMC wool skeins as listed in colour key
(7 colours)
   Use 1 whole strand of wool per stitching
thread

10-count antique deluxe canvas
   Design size: 14.5 x 12in (36.5 x 30cm)
   Canvas size: 19 x 16in (47.5 x 40cm)

Backing fabric: 19 x 16in (47.5 x 40cm)
Chair seat pad: 14.5 x 12 x 1.5in
   (36.5 x 30 x 4cm) foam
Braid: 3.5yds (3.15m), allowing a little
   extra if loops are needed for tassels
Tassels/tag ends: 4 (see page 122–3)

See page 122 for making-up instructions

KEY TO COLOURS (*showing DMC brand
number, general colour name and number of
skeins required*):

⬛	7108	Red	(1)
⬜	7192	Pink	(1)
▨	7424	Light green	(4)
▨	7428	Dark green	(3)
⬜	7724	Beige	(12)
⬛	7535	Dark brown	(1)
⬜	Blanc	White	(2)

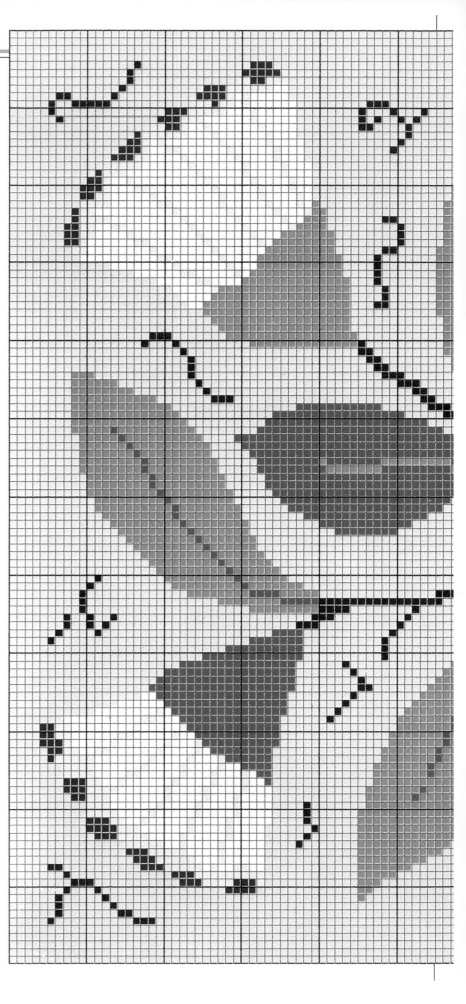

58

RED/BLUE AND GOLD CHAIR SEAT COVER

MATERIALS:

DMC wool and stranded cotton skeins as listed in colour key (2 colours)
    Use 1 whole strand of wool/12 strands of cotton per stitching thread

10-count antique deluxe canvas
    Design size: 14.5 x 12in (36.5 x 30cm)
    Canvas size: 19 x 16in (47.5 x 40cm)

Backing fabric: 19 x 16in (47.5 x 40cm)
Chair seat pad: 14.5 x 12 x 1.5in
    (36.5 x 30 x 4cm) foam
Braid: 3.5yds (3.15m), allowing a little
    extra if loops are needed for tassels
Tassels/tag ends: 4 (see page 122–3)

See page 122 for making-up instructions

KEY TO COLOURS (*showing DMC brand number, general colour name and number of skeins required*):

    WOOL

★   7108   Red   (20)

    or

■   7319   Blue   (20)

    COTTON

▨   729   Gold   (15)

★ *as shown in illustration on page 53*

FLORAL RUG

MATERIALS:

6 chair seat cover panels
Backing fabric: 24 x 43.5in (60 x 109cm)
Fringe: 48in (120cm)

See page 126 for making-up instructions

Framed Spring Panels

Inspired by a French Book of Hours

THE OCCUPATIONS OF the months of April and May from a French Book of Hours dating from the fifteenth century provided the inspiration for this project. In most cases a Book of Hours opened with a calendar of the Church's saints' and feast days and it was usual for each month to be accompanied by a scene of the labour or pleasure appropriate to it. These varied from area to area, but generally followed the same pattern: January, feasting; February, sitting around a fire; March, pruning; April, planting trees or picking flowers; May, hawking; June, haymaking; July, harvesting; August, threshing; September, wine-making; October, sowing; November, boar-hunting; December, collecting wood. In some cases the twelve signs of the zodiac were also included.

In this manuscript, scenes of courtly rather than country life are depicted: April's elegant dalliance among the wild flowers and May's cheerful hawking party. Hawking was a very fashionable sport for men and women in the fourteenth and fifteenth centuries; the birds were carried on the wrist and trained to swoop on game, kill it and then return to their owners. They were much prized and often had elaborately embroidered hoods and jesses.

The wealthy inhabitants of fifteenth-century France were much concerned with fashion and it is easy to see the appeal of secular scenes such as these in a highly valuable decorated and gold-clasped Book of Hours.

An illumination depicting the activities of April (picking flowers, above) and May (hawking, below), taken from a French Book of Hours produced in the fifteenth century.

THESE GENTEEL SCENES arc by far the most attractive calendar illustrations that I came across in my research, since many others tend to concentrate on more lowly, practical country pursuits, such as pig slaughtering! Interestingly, the artist appears to have had much more of a feel for the detailing of the horses and the jolly little dogs than the faces of the nobility who have nothing better to do than pick posies and exercise their hawks.

Set in realistic landscapes, both paintings are far more suitable for framing than the purely decorative designs used elsewhere for more flexible items such as cushions. A very simple, quite wide frame was chosen, in keeping with the style of the period. Never detract from a design with a fussy frame or one which obviously clashes stylistically.

'Ennewed your colour/Is like the daisy flower/After the April shower./Star of the morrow gray,/The blossom on the spray,/The freshest flower of May;/Maidenly demure,/Of womanhood the lure;/Wherefore, I make you sure.' To Mistress Isabel Pennell,
JOHN SKELTON

APRIL FRAMED PANEL CHART

MATERIALS:

DMC wool skeins as listed in colour key (25 colours)
　　Use 1 whole strand of wool per stitching thread

12-count antique deluxe canvas
　　Design size: 19.5 x 11in (49 x 27.5cm)
　　Canvas size: 24 x 15in (60 x 37.5cm)

Backing board and frame (see page 128 for suppliers)

See page 124 for making-up instructions

KEY TO COLOURS *(showing DMC brand number, general colour name and number of skeins required):*

	7472	Yellow	(1)
	7845	Dark ginger	(5)
	7107	Red	(1)
	7950	Light pink	(2)
	7165	Mid-pink	(1)
	7167	Very dark pink	(1)
	7798	Mid-blue	(2)
	7318	Dark blue	(3)
	7307	Very dark blue	(1)
	7370	Light green	(3)
	7396	Mid-green	(2)
	7359	Very dark green	(1)
	7424	Light olive green	(2)
	7426	Grass green	(7)
	7377	Dark olive green	(1)
	7724	Sand	(1)

	7162	Beige	(3)		7459	Dark rust	(1)		7622	Mid-grey	(1)
	7455	Light ginger	(2)		7535	Dark brown	(1)		7510	Off-white	(2)
	7525	Mid-brown	(1)		7624	Dark grey	(1)		Ecru	Ecru	(1)

MAY FRAMED PANEL CHART

MATERIALS:

DMC wool skeins as listed in colour key (25 colours)
Use 1 whole strand of wool per stitching thread

12-count antique deluxe canvas
Design size: 19.5 x 11in (49 x 27.5cm)
Canvas size: 24 x 15in (60 x 37.5cm)

Backing board and frame (see page 128 for suppliers)

See page 124 for making-up instructions

KEY TO COLOURS (*showing DMC brand number, general colour name and number of skeins required*):

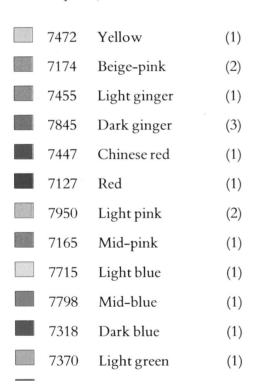

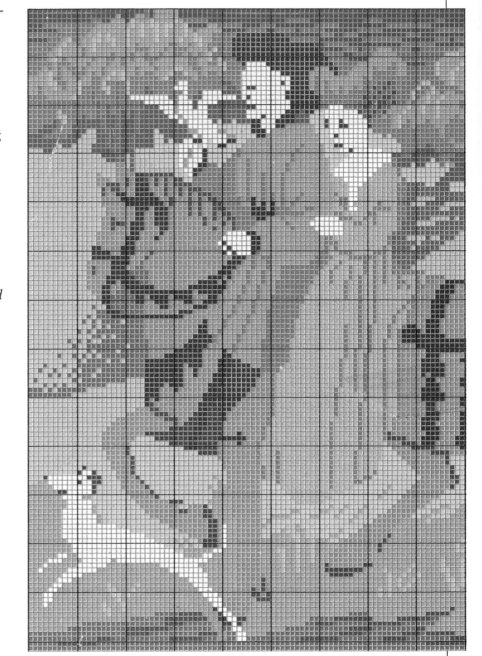

	7472	Yellow	(1)					
	7174	Beige-pink	(2)					
	7455	Light ginger	(1)					
	7845	Dark ginger	(3)					
	7447	Chinese red	(1)					
	7127	Red	(1)					
	7950	Light pink	(2)					
	7165	Mid-pink	(1)					
	7715	Light blue	(1)					
	7798	Mid-blue	(1)					
	7318	Dark blue	(1)					
	7370	Light green	(1)					
	7396	Mid-green	(2)					
	7359	Very dark green	(2)					
	7426	Mid-olive green	(5)					
	7739	Light biscuit	(2)					
	7511	Dark beige	(2)		7467	Dark brown	(1)	7273	Mid-grey	(1)
	7525	Mid-brown	(3)		7535	Very dark brown	(1)	7510	Off-white	(4)
	7459	Rust brown	(1)		7622	Charcoal grey	(1)	Ecru	Ecru	(1)

Pair of Bird Cushions and Posy Pin Cushion

Inspired by the Life of Alexander the Great

AN ILLUSTRATION OF the Court of Alexander the Great, from a manuscript made in Flanders *c.* 1470–80 for Engelbert of Nassau, whose coat of arms is displayed within the border decoration.

As they became increasingly literate, European medieval nobles developed a voracious appetite for literature. Aside from their devotional books, they loved the stories of myth and historical legend: romantic accounts of the ancient heroes and battles—of Alexander the Great, the Fall of Troy, Charlemagne, and King Arthur. In addition, the songs and stories of the medieval troubadours—the 'Roman de la Rose' and the 'Chanson de Roland' —were written down and thus became more widely disseminated. Richly ornamented and illustrated copies of these became important acquisitions for a nobleman's library.

This manuscript is a French translation of the *Life of Alexander the Great* by Quintus Curtius Rufus. The exploits of this ancient king of Macedonia, who founded an empire in the fourth century BC, had been described in the writings of Plutarch and Herodotus, and his military prowess clearly caught the medieval imagination. What has been illustrated here is a contemporary, not an ancient scene. This court is probably very similar to that of Engelbert of Nassau: a Gothic hall, musicians, a jester, with the most important members of the court up on a dais and under a canopy. Wealth is conspicuously displayed by the ar- and silver tankards, candlesticks and wall-hangings and the richly brocaded clothes.

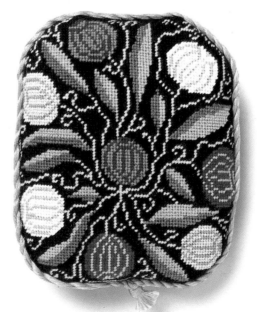

An illumination showing the Court of Alexander the Great, taken from the Life of Alexander the Great, *made for Engelbert of Nassau c. 1470–80.*

lexandre
fist sumptu
eusement
mettre en
sepulture
les gens de guerre quil avoit
perdu en chassant le roy darie
et distribua .xim.m markz

aux auures compaignons
de son armee dont la pluspt
des cheuaulx fut perdue · et
mesmes ceulz qui demoure
rent par la pluye et grant
challeur se morfondirent.
Toute la proye quon auoit
deuant assamblee de la cite

THIS ILLUSTRATED PAGE positively teems with life, so much so that it provided inspiration not only for a pair of cushions but also for a pin cushion. One of the designs centres on a hawk-like bird surrounded by huge succulent-looking strawberries, quite life-like but totally out of scale. His partner, who sports beautiful parrot-like plumage, is also surrounded by enormous blooms.

The composition lends itself to quite compact, square cushions but if larger ones were required they could be made by adding a fabric border around the canvas; one of rich greens or blues would create a perfect frame for the design. Individually, they could be used to upholster the seat of a special chair.

'The throstle with her warbling;/The starling with her brabling;/The rook, with the osprey/That putteth fishes to a fray;/And the dainty curlew,/With the turtledove most true.' Philip Sparrow, JOHN SKELTON

'Holly hath birds, a full fair flock,/The nightingale, the popinjay, the gentle lark./Good Ivy, what birds hast thou?/None but the howlet that cries: "How, how!"' Holly and his Merry Men, ANON.

PARAKEET CUSHION CHART

MATERIALS:

DMC wool skeins as listed in colour key (14 colours)
  Use 1 whole strand of wool per stitching thread

12-count antique deluxe canvas
  Design size: 12 x 12.5in (30 x 31.5cm)
  Canvas size: 16 x 16.5in (40 x 41.5cm)

Backing fabric: 16 x 16.5in (40 x 41.5cm)
Braid: 1.4yds (1.25m)
Feather pad: 12 x 12in (30 x 30cm)

See page 122 for making-up instructions

KEY TO COLOURS (*showing DMC brand number,*
general colour name and number of skeins required):

	7503	Light gold	(12)
	7472	Yellow	(1)
	7447	Chinese red	(1)
	7650	Blue	(3)
	7596	Mid-teal blue	(2)
	7860	Dark teal blue	(1)
	7297	Dark blue	(2)
	7542	Light green	(2)
	7541	Mid-green	(6)
	7701	Dark green	(2)
	7525	Mid-brown	(1)
	7459	Rust brown	(2)
	7309	Blue-black	(1)
	7510	Off-white	(4)

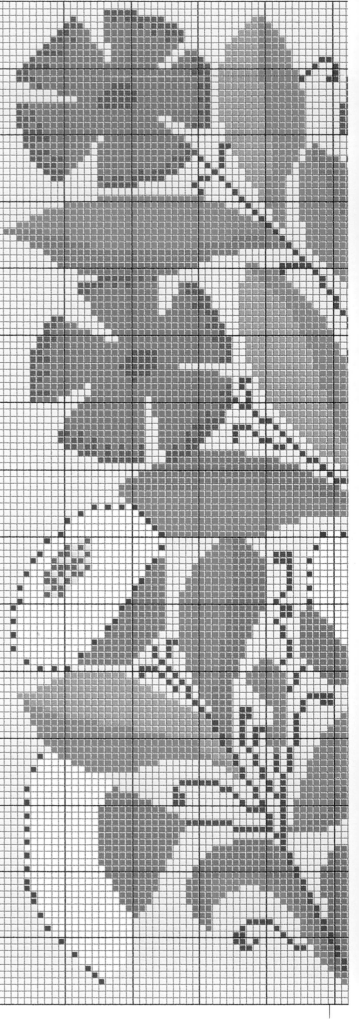

HAWK CUSHION CHART

MATERIALS:

DMC wool skeins as listed in colour key (15 colours)
  Use 1 whole strand of wool per stitching thread

12-count antique deluxe canvas
  Design size: 12 x 12.5in (30 x 31.5cm)
  Canvas size: 16 x 16.5in (40 x 41.5cm)

Backing fabric: 16 x 16.5in (40 x 41.5cm)
Braid: 1.4yds (1.25m)
Feather pad: 12 x 12in (30 x 30cm)

See page 122 for making-up instructions

KEY TO COLOURS (*showing DMC brand number,
general colour name and number of skeins required*):

	7503	Light gold	(12)
	7472	Yellow	(1)
	7494	Ochre	(1)
	7920	Strawberry red	(4)
	7447	Chinese red	(1)
	7595	Mid-blue	(2)
	7297	Dark blue	(1)
	7541	Light green	(3)
	7701	Mid-green	(5)
	7429	Dark green	(1)
	7525	Light brown	(1)
	7459	Rust brown	(2)
	7538	Very dark brown	(4)
	Noir	Black	(1)
	7510	Off-white	(2)

F OR THE PIN CUSHION, the tiny floral design encapsulated within the opening letter of this text caught my eye because of the lovely colour combinations set against a dramatic black background.

Worked on larger canvas, this design would make an attractive oval pouf, made up in the same way as the pin cushion: half canvas, half backing fabric. Instead of fine, hand–twisted cord (see page 124), it could be trimmed with really chunky braid, tied in an extravagant knot to one side.

'For to the green wood I must go/To pick the nut and also the sloe,/To pick the red rose and the thyme/To strew my mother's bower and mine.' Gil Brenton, ANON.

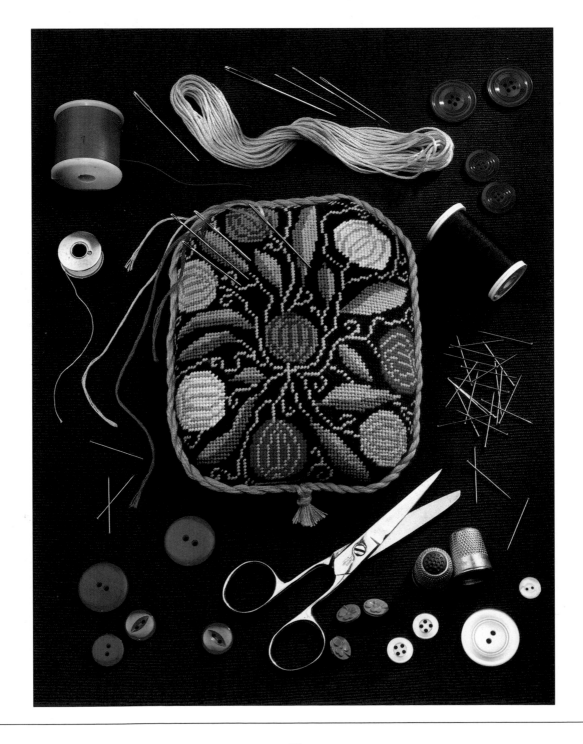

POSY PIN CUSHION CHART

MATERIALS:

DMC stranded cotton skeins as listed in colour key (11 colours)
Use 6 strands of cotton per stitching thread

18-count antique deluxe canvas
Design size: 5 x 6in (12.5 x 15cm)
Canvas size: 8 x 9in (20 x 22.5cm)

Backing fabric: 8 x 9in (20 x 22.5cm)
Stuffing
Extra cotton to make braid
(see page 124)

See page 123 for making-up instructions

KEY TO COLOURS *(showing DMC brand number, general colour name and number of skeins required):*

745	Light yellow	(1)
834	Gold	(1)
729	Dark yellow	(1)
919	Rust	(1)
950	Peach	(1)
407	Dark peach	(1)
322	Blue	(1)
311	Dark blue	(1)
992	Light green	(1)
991	Dark green	(1)
Noir	Black	(4)

Woodland Deer Hanging

Inspired by the Livre de Chasse

HUNTING WAS THE SPORT of kings and nobles and the greatest quarry of all was a stag. Stags of venerable age, does and fawns are charmingly illustrated in this page from the *Livre de Chasse*, the 'Book of Hunting', by Gaston, Count de Foix and Viscount de Béarn. An aristocrat, who was also a soldier and minor poet, he married Agnes, the sister of the King of Navarre, and was clearly in a position to experience the best hunting that France had to offer. This manuscript would have been made shortly after his death in 1391 (of a stroke while on the hunting field).

Hunting game was carefully controlled during the medieval period, and poaching even the smallest animal was an offence punishable by death. Gaston de Foix, or Gaston Phoebus as he was also called, described in detail how to find, hunt and catch such animals as the hart, hare, buck, roe, wild boar, wolf, badger, cat, otter, reindeer, chamois, bear and rabbit. He also gives an exposition on the merits and training of different types of hunting dogs.

The book was a great success in English as well as French, translated by Edward, Duke of York, while imprisoned in Pevensey Castle between 1406 and 1413 for plotting to assassinate the king.

The families of deer in this miniature are carefully observed but their habitat has a characteristically medieval confusion of scale: stunted trees set against over-large clumps of wild flowers. Unwilling to leave the sky a plain blue, the artist has elaborated it with whorls of delicate golden tracery; the expenditure of so much time in ornamentation was commensurate with the value placed on such a work.

A depiction of stag hunting, taken from the Livre de Chasse *by Gaston, Count de Foix and Viscount de Béarn, produced in the late fourteenth century.*

ROM THIS INCREDIBLY DETAILED woodland scene I took the family group from one corner to create a rectangular design. Just add simple cord loops to the upper edge, and hang it from a pole in true medieval fashion. (For alternative methods see page 125.)

The doe and fawn are so sensitively portrayed that they make an attractive scene by themselves; this area alone could be worked to create a charming little picture which could then be framed. When taking extracts from a design in this way always remember to add extra rows of stitches to each edge so that none of the design is lost in framing or making-up.

'To see the deer draw to the dale/And leave the hills high,/And
shadow them in the leaves green/Under the greenwood tree.'
Robin Hood and the Monk, ANON.

WOODLAND DEER
HANGING CHART

MATERIALS:

DMC wool skeins as listed in colour key
(16 colours)
    Use 1 whole strand of wool per stitching
thread

12-count antique deluxe canvas
    Design size: 15 x 19.5in (37.5 x 49cm)
    Canvas size: 20 x 24in (50 x 60cm)

Backing fabric: 20 x 24in (50 x 60cm)
Braid (for loops): approx. 16in (40cm)

See page 125 for making-up instructions

KEY TO COLOURS *(showing DMC brand
number, general colour name and number of
skeins required):*

	7579	Light yellow	(2)
	7472	Yellow	(6)
	7833	Ginger	(2)
	7457	Rust	(1)
	7303	Chinese red	(6)
	7297	Dark blue	(7)
	7424	Light green	(2)
	7426	Mid-green	(3)
	7367	Bright green	(5)
	7396	Blue-green	(2)
	7359	Dark olive green	(5)
	7724	Beige	(1)
	7845	Honey brown	(1)
	7467	Dark red-brown	(4)
	7469	Very dark brown	(3)
	7538	Brown-black	(5)

Floral Work-box Top

Inspired by the
Soane Book of Hours

THIS FOLIO IS from a Book of Hours made in Ghent or Bruges *c.* 1500. It comes from the section containing the seven Penitential Psalms, which is accompanied by a litany of the saints. The beautiful spring and early summer flowers scattered around the border of the miniature belie the powerful nature of the subject matter.

In the illumination on the folio facing this, St Gregory, newly elected Pope in 590, heads a procession of hooded flagellants, clerics and ordinary people making their way to St Peter's to pray for the cessation of the plague in the city of Rome. Victims lie heaped on the ground as the Pope leads the way over the Tiber clutching a picture of the Virgin Mary. Also on the opposite page, an apparition of an angel holding a bloody sword appears on a pinnacle of the citadel.

No two Books of Hours are the same, each one a slightly different combination of prayers, psalms, calendars and illuminated miniatures and initials. The depiction of the saints varies from area to area and at different periods, but it would seem that a patron regarded the saints he chose for inclusion almost as talismans, offering protection against particular ills and dangers. Thus, St Gregory might well have been included to inspire prayers asking for relief from the plagues and diseases that were still rife when the Book of Hours was made.

An illumination of the Procession of St Gregory, taken from the
Soane Book of Hours, made in Ghent or Bruges in the late
fifteenth or early sixteenth century.

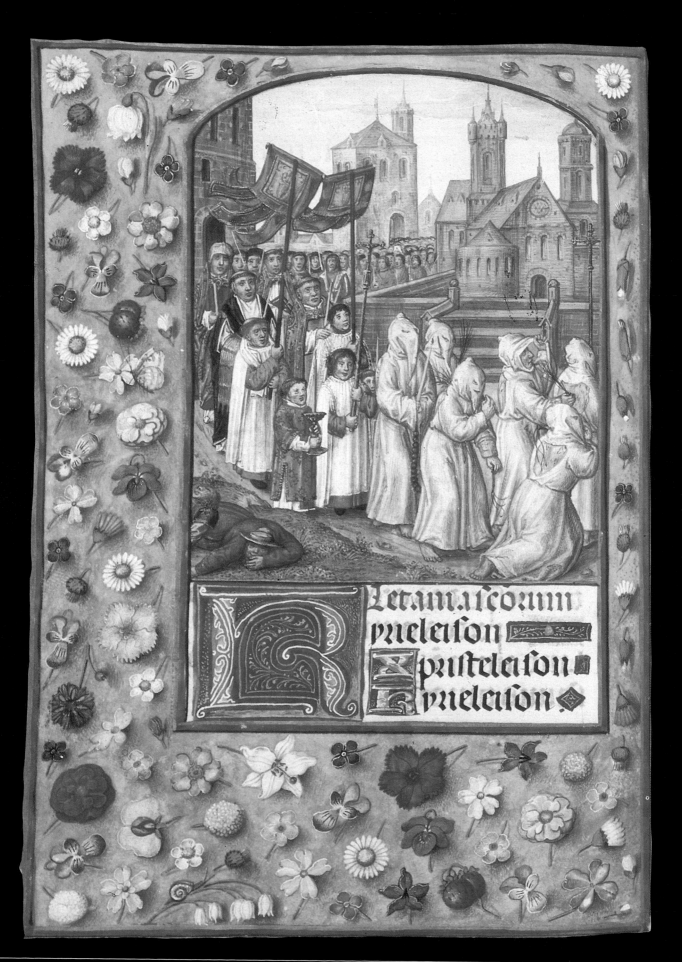

THE USE OF SCATTERED FLOWERS to create a border is often seen in medieval manuscripts and provides a really pretty subject for needlepoint. I particularly liked the pastel colours of this border but it was difficult to choose which area of the whole to use; it was the lily at the top of the design that decided it. You could experiment with different colourways. Darker, bolder colours might be more appropriate if the box is to receive a lot of wear as they soil less noticeably; a dark wood box will blend in best.

The design has been set into a custom-made box (see page 124), but any number of small items could be made by extracting single flowers from the chart: small pin or herb cushions, little round box lids, and insets for cards.

> *'Plainly, I cannot praise;*
> *Ye be, as I devine,*
> *The pretty primrose,*
> *The goodly columbine.*
>
> *With marjoram gentle,*
> *The flower of goodlihead,*
> *Embroidered the mantle*
> *Is of your maidenhead.'*

To Mistress Margery Wentworth, JOHN SKELTON

' "I love a flower of sweet odour." / "Marjoram gentle, or lavender?" / "Columbine, marigolds of sweet flavour?" / "Nay, nay, let be! / Is none of them / That liketh me." '
ROSES, ANON.

FLORAL WORK-BOX TOP CHART

MATERIALS:

DMC stranded cotton skeins as listed in colour key (15 colours)
  Use 9 strands of cotton per stitching thread

14-count antique deluxe canvas
  Design size: 12 x 8.5in (30 x 21.5cm)
  Canvas size: 16 x 12in (40 x 30cm)

Work-box pad and base (see page 128 for suppliers)

See page 124 for making-up instructions

KEY TO COLOURS *(showing DMC brand number, general colour name and number of skeins required):*

754	Light yellow	(2)
783	Mid-gold	(22)
976	Dark gold	(4)
920	Red-orange	(1)
761	Light pink	(3)
3328	Mid-pink	(2)
3740	Purple	(1)
3756	Very light blue	(2)
3761	Light blue	(1)
562	Green	(2)
613	Beige	(2)
975	Dark golden brown	(2)
Noir	Black	(1)
451	Grey	(1)
Ecru	Ecru	(6)

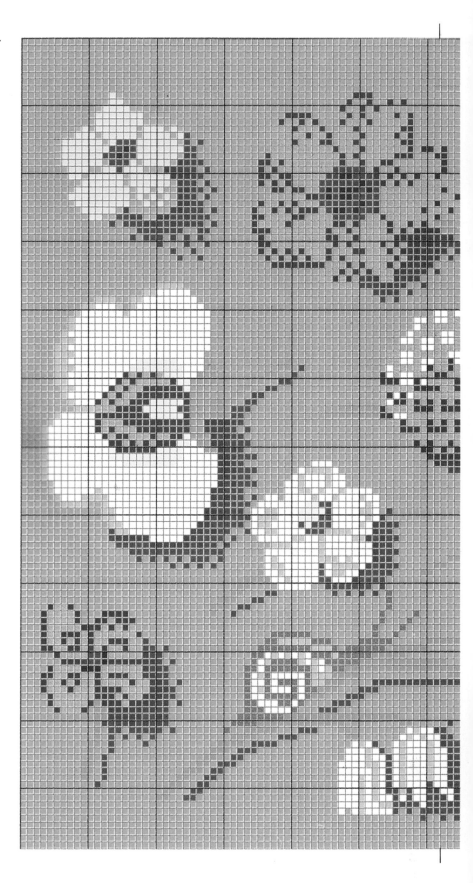

Fox and Raven Firescreen

Inspired by Spiegel der Weisheit

I HAVE BASED this project very closely on an illustration from an Austrian manuscript, dating from the first quarter of the fifteenth century, which was a collection of moral tales by the Apostle of the Slovenians, St Cyril of Thessalonika. This is a German translation, and although the original was probably written in Greek, it is only otherwise known by its Latin title, *Speculum Sapiente*, 'The Mirror of Wisdom'.

A miniature illustrates each tale, the cast of characters designed to appeal to a medieval audience: maidens, unicorns, goats, dragons, peacocks and whales. In this story of the Fox and the Raven, an aged fox goes in search of a teacher. He finds a knowledgeable raven (symbol of death), but proves himself wiser than his tutor when he rejects the raven's argument that he is wise enough already; as long as you are alive you should strive to better yourself, he counters.

The fox made frequent appearances in medieval literature. He was a powerful and dominant figure in the enduringly popular *Fables* of Aesop, characterizing all that is cunning, sly and devious. A favourite medieval epic tale, 'Reynard the Fox', endows the animal with the same character. The fox also occasionally appears amongst the marginal illustrations of satirical manuscripts, dressed as a cleric or monk and behaving in a less than pious manner.

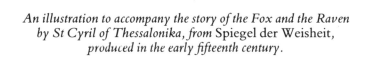

An illustration to accompany the story of the Fox and the Raven by St Cyril of Thessalonika, from Spiegel der Weisheit, *produced in the early fifteenth century.*

O F ALL THE CREATURES in the manuscripts that I have studied, this little fox looking up into the tree is my favourite. He has been so lovingly painted that when you look at him through a magnifying glass you feel that you could almost stroke his fur. I took the liberty of removing his friend from the design, who appears to have been overcome by the effort of trying to reach the raven, also beautifully and realistically painted. Set against this life-like scene there is one of the most exotic skies that I have ever seen, as dramatic as Van Gogh's 'Starry Night'.

This is a design which comes with its own 'frame' worked in stitches and so, besides being set in a firescreen, it would also be ideally suited for use as a wall hanging.

*'The monk with all his strength heaved/Until at last the wolf he
see-d/. . . Well and sorely was he thrashed,/with staves and
spears was he bashed./The fox had duped him, with his guile.'*
The Fox and the Wolf, ANON.

FOX AND RAVEN FIRESCREEN CHART

MATERIALS:

DMC wool skeins as listed in key (16 colours)
    Use 1 whole strand of wool per stitching thread

12-count antique deluxe canvas
    Design size: 25 x 21in (62.5 x 52.5cm)
    Canvas size: 30 x 26in (75 x 65cm)

Firescreen (see page 128 for suppliers)

See page 124 for making-up instructions

KEY TO COLOURS *(showing DMC brand number, general colour name and number of skeins required):*

	7503	Pale yellow	(3)
	7472	Mid-yellow	(2)
	7724	Sand	(1)
	7845	Ginger	(2)
	7184	Red	(9)
	7234	Mauve	(1)
	7336	Dark blue	(2)
	7542	Pale green	(12)
	7702	Grey-green	(3)
	7541	Mid-green	(7)
	7429	Very dark green	(17)
	7391	Khaki	(3)
	7535	Very dark brown	(6)
	Noir	Black	(1)
	7713	Charcoal grey	(2)
	7510	Off-white	(1)

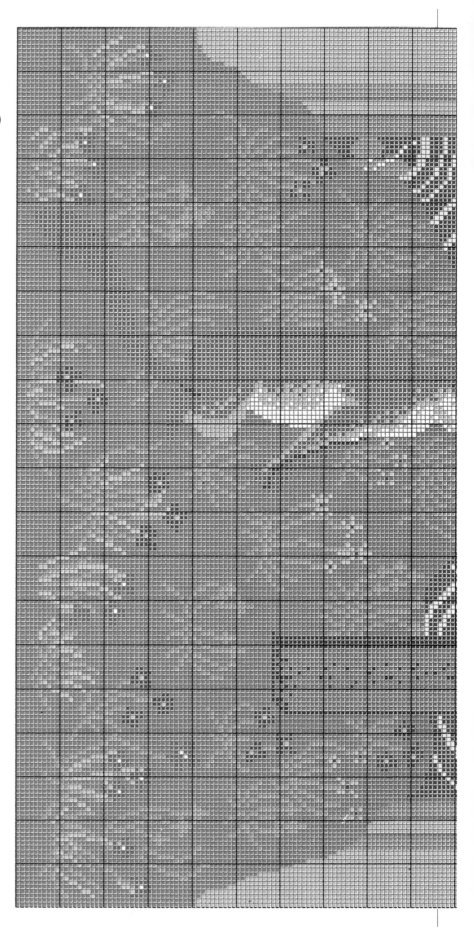

Lattice Box Stool

Inspired by the Soane Book of Hours

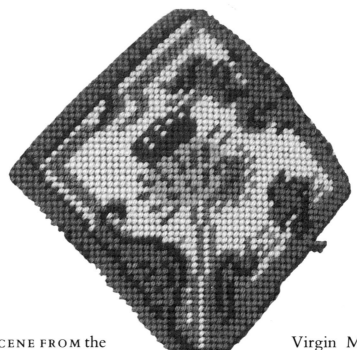

THIS SCENE FROM the of the Visitation. It shows her cousin, shortly after the many years of failing to conceive, is pregnant by her husband Virgin Mary's life is Mary meeting Elizabeth, Annunciation. Elizabeth, after Zacharias, a high priest at the temple. Her child was to be John the Baptist, born six months before Christ, although in this miniature Mary is also depicted as heavily pregnant.

Behind is a Flemish rural landscape with the house of Zacharias portrayed as being in the most up-to-date Gothic style, with a stepped gable, Gothic tracery, patterned roof tiles and elaborate chimney.

The lattice design also has a very Gothic feel to it: the twig-like divisions sprouting leafy crockets, an ornamental addition ubiquitous in Gothic architecture.

However, inspiration for the design is clearly in the medieval garden, where trellises covered in climbing flowers and surrounding 'flowery meads' were one of the most popular forms of planting. Some lines of Chaucer (from his translation of the 'Roman de la Rose') give a clear description:

> *'There sprang the violet all new,*
> *And fresh periwinkle, rich of hue,*
> *And flowers yellow, white and red;*
> *Such plenty grew there never in mead.'*

An illumination of the Visitation, taken from the Soane Book of Hours, *made in Ghent or Bruges in the late fifteenth or early sixteenth century.*

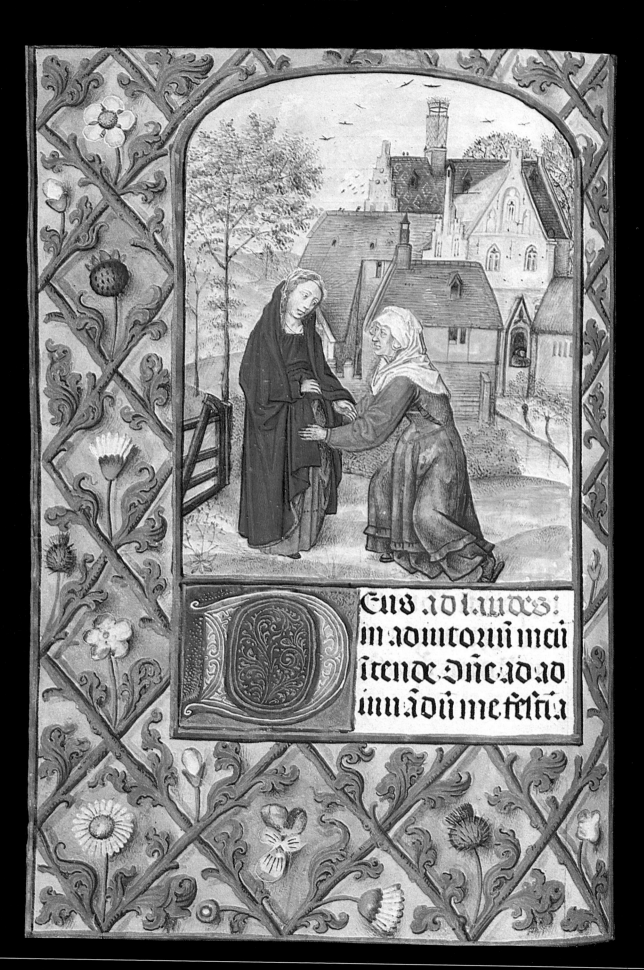

eus ad laudes:
m adutonu mei
itende dñe ad ad
iuu adiu me festia

THE RUSTIC TRELLIS of this border is quite an unusual geometric device for a medieval manuscript but it creates a lovely design, each diamond framing a different type of flower, thistle, bud or fruit. I have recreated two main panels from the page, and in order to make the box stool in one piece the instructions and flat-plan on page 126 should be followed, as the repeats are worked in specific directions.

The top section can easily be isolated, to make a cushion. Alternatively, the design can be separated into its two panels, enabling you to work it in half or repeat it endlessly if required, perhaps to make a pelmet.

The adventurous needlepointer might like to tackle a rug using large canvas and working a number of panels which could then be stitched together (see page 126, top).

*'Now was there made fast by the tower wall/A garden fair,
and in the corner set/An arbour green, with stakes long
and small.'* The Nightingale's Song, KING JAMES I
OF SCOTLAND

LATTICE BOX STOOL CHART

MATERIALS:

DMC wool skeins as listed in colour key (15 colours)
  Use 1 whole strand of wool per stitching thread

10-count antique deluxe canvas
  Design size (project worked as one piece): 25 x 25in
  (62 x 62cm)
  Canvas size: 30 x 30in (75 x 75cm)

Box stool pad and base (see page 128 for suppliers)

See page 126 for making-up instructions

KEY TO COLOURS *(showing DMC brand number, general colour name and number of skeins required):*

	7579	Light yellow	(16)
	7455	Gold	(1)
	7508	Ginger	(18)
	7447	Dark rust	(9)
	7200	Light pink	(1)
	7758	Dark pink	(1)
	7715	Light grey-blue	(1)
	7802	Aqua	(1)
	7424	Light green	(7)
	7377	Dark green	(5)
	7511	Beige	(4)
	7234	Dark grey	(3)
	7535	Very dark brown	(1)
	7300	Light grey	(6)
	Ecru	Ecru	(3)

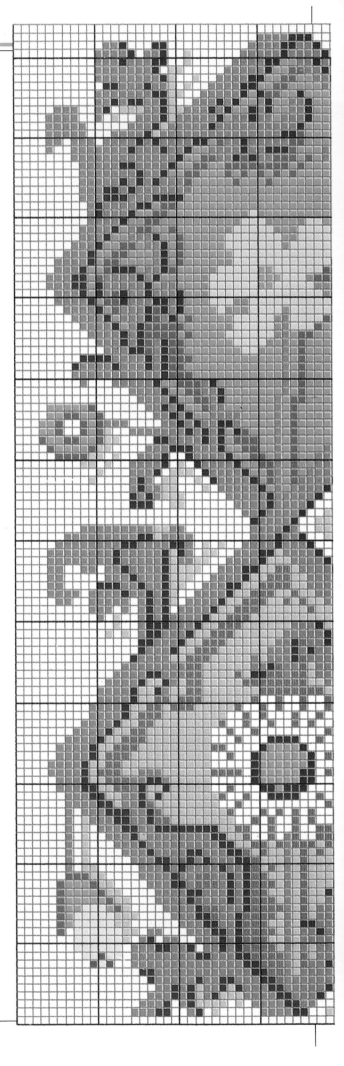

Ivy-leaf Picture Frame

Inspired by the
St Louis Psalter

THIS PAGE IS TAKEN from the earliest manuscript used in this book, the *Psalter of St Louis*, made in 1253. King of France from the age of eleven, Louis IX was canonized in 1297, only twenty-seven years after his death. He was considered to be a model Christian ruler: mild, just and chivalrous. He went on a Crusade to Egypt and Palestine, and on his return built the magnificent Sainte-Chapelle in Paris to enshrine the relics he had brought back with him: fragments of the True Cross and the Crown of Thorns. He died from the plague in Tunis, while on his second Crusade.

A Psalter was the most common book of private devotion until the Book of Hours became more popular. It contained all the psalms and additional poetic passages from the Old and New Testaments. The scene on this page is from the Old Testament and illustrates a passage from Genesis chapter 18, in which three men appear before Abraham. He recognizes them as angels and offers them food and hospitality, and they proceed to prophesy the birth of Isaac to Abraham and his wife Sarah. In the light of the New Testament, King Louis would have seen the three angels as symbolic of the Trinity and the whole story as a prefiguration of the Annunciation of the birth of Christ.

This illumination, executed in the bold and schematic style characteristic of Gothic work, shows two scenes of the story within a single frame, the oak tree used as a dividing line between Abraham meeting the angels outside his tent and then offering them food inside. In the background, a splendid Gothic cathedral has been reproduced in preference to the historically correct Middle Eastern desert.

Abraham and the Three Angels, taken from the St Louis Psalter, *made in 1253 for King Louis IX of France.*

ALTHOUGH THIS IS an early illumination, executed in a rather primitive style, the lovely combination of terracotta, gold and indigo in the border attracted me. The ivy leaf repeat, broken up by the rather cuddly monsters intertwined at each corner, presented a ready-made frame shape which just needed a little adjustment to create a symmetrical design. It is worked in silky cotton thread to give maximum depth of colour. Detailed making-up instructions are to be found on page 124.

'Ivy is green with colour bright;/Of all trees best she is;/And that I prove well now by right:/Veni, coronaberis.' Ivy, Chief of Trees, ANON.

IVY-LEAF PICTURE FRAME CHART

MATERIALS:

DMC stranded cotton skeins as listed in colour key (8 colours)
Use 6 strands of cotton per stitching thread

18-count antique deluxe canvas
Design size: 12.5 x 12.5in x 1.5in
(31.5 x 31.5 x 4cm)
Canvas size: 16 x 16in
(40 x 40cm)

Stiff card: 12.5 x 12.5in
(31.5 x 31.5cm)

Mirror or picture

See page 124–5 for making-up instructions

KEY TO COLOURS *(showing DMC brand number, general colour name and number of skeins required):*

	744	Yellow	(1)
	783	Gold	(7)
	919	Rust	(2)
	311	Dark blue	(5)
	738	Beige	(3)
	434	Mid-brown	(3)
	938	Very dark brown	(8)
	Ecru	Ecru	(6)

Vine-work Glasses Case

Inspired by the Historia Naturalis

THE TEXT OF THIS MANUSCRIPT of the *Historia Naturalis* was originally written in the first century AD by Pliny the Elder and comprised thirty-seven books of Natural History. It was an encyclopedia of knowledge of the known universe—of the earth, men, plants, animals, medicines and arts—and remained a prime source of information right up to the Middle Ages.

Texts by the ancient classical authors were avidly collected by the humanists in Renaissance Italy for their splendid libraries. The booksellers of Venice, Florence and Siena met the demand with a quantity of manuscripts of texts by Greek and Roman writers, such as the *Dialogues* of Plato, Ovid's *Metamorphoses*, Aesop's *Fables*, Virgil's *Aeneid* and Livy's *Histories*. In the ornamentation of these a conscious effort was made to get away from Gothic naturalism, which was associated with Christian works. Instead, they used this abstract interlacing, a revival of the Romanesque decoration which they believed to be classical in spirit. It is often called white vine work.

The initial is historiated, the term used to describe illuminated initials that include small pictures. Entrapped within the interlacing is a collection of beasts, both real and mythical. The fact that the mythical dragon seems to be walking away from the lion, the elephant and the leopard perhaps indicates that he is pointing the way to an alternative, more spiritual, understanding of the world.

A detail of an initial-letter illumination, taken from a copy of
Pliny the Elder's Historia Naturalis *made c.1460.*

THIS LABYRINTH of twisting vines just goes on and on, intertwining for what appears to be eternity. I had not only to prune them down to a single panel but also to balance out the design, which has the characteristic medieval disregard for symmetry.

The glasses case may be made either by stitching two identical pieces and sewing them together or by backing one stitched panel with a piece of appropriate fabric cut to the same shape (see page 123).

The strong combination of maroon, indigo and bottle green makes this design suitable for many other larger upholstered projects where it could be used in conjunction with velvets of similar shades.

'And see the fresh flowers how they spring; /
Full is mine heart of revel and solace!'
The Cock and the Hen, GEOFFREY CHAUCER

VINE-WORK GLASSES CASE CHART

MATERIALS:

DMC stranded cotton skeins as listed in colour key (7 colours)
   Use 6 strands of cotton per stitching thread

18-count antique deluxe canvas
   Design size: 3.5 x 3.5in (9 x 19cm)
   Canvas size: 7.5 x 11in (19 x 27.5cm)

Backing fabric (if working single-sided version): 7.5 x 11in (19 x 27.5cm)
Lining fabric: 11 x 11in (27.5 x 27.5cm)
Extra cotton to make braid (see page 124)

See page 123 for making-up instructions

KEY TO COLOURS *(showing DMC brand number, general colour name and number of skeins required, single-/double-sided):*

	833	Gold	(1/2)
	814	Maroon	(1/2)
	311	Blue	(2/3)
	561	Green	(1/2)
	642	Beige	(1/2)
	3031	Dark brown	(1/2)
	Ecru	Ecru	(5/9)

Crusader Cushion

Inspired by a
history of the Crusades

THIS IS AN ILLUMINATION from a history of the Crusades, made in France and dating from the late fourteenth or early fifteenth century. The scene it depicts had therefore taken place at least 250 years earlier, when the actual Crusaders would have worn cloaks and tunics bearing the symbol of the cross.

The knights riding so calmly into battle represent Count Godefroy de Bouillon with a group of his soldiers. Count Godefroy led one of the five armies of the First Crusade, which left France for the Holy Land late in the summer of 1096 to deliver Jerusalem from the hands of the Turkish infidel and restore it to Christian rule. Godefroy was famed for his extreme piety, and when the Crusaders returned in 1099 he was elected an Advocate of the Holy Sepulchre, although he refused the title of King of Jerusalem. All his men were promised a place in heaven, as soldiers of Christ, for their part in liberating the city.

The immaculate caparisons of the horses as they prance over a flowered field, the crisply unfurling banners and the tall plumed helmets of the Crusaders bear little comparison to the harsh realities of fever, thirst and starvation suffered by the real Crusaders.

Godefroy de Bouillon leads his men into the Crusades, taken from a history of the Crusades produced in France during the late fourteenth or early fifteenth century.

T HIS SCENE is a perfect composition as it stands, requiring none of the little bits of artistic licence which were necessary to create pleasing designs elsewhere in the book. It has a wonderful vigour which almost bursts out of the page, the knights' lances and flags actually piercing the upper border in a number of places and some of the horses' hooves crashing into the lower one. The bold colouring gives further impact to the design, making it an ideal project to work in wool on a large scale.

*'A Knight there was, and that a worthy man,/That from the time
that he first began/To ride out, he loved the chivalry,/Truth
and honour, freedom and courtesy.'* Canterbury Tales,
GEOFFREY CHAUCER

CRUSADER CUSHION CHART

MATERIALS:

DMC wool skeins as listed in colour key
(11 colours)
   Use 1 whole strand of wool per stitching thread

10-count antique deluxe canvas
   Design size: 19.5 x 21.5in (49 x 54cm)
   Canvas size: 24 x 25in (60 x 62.5cm)

Backing fabric: 24 x 25in (60 x 62.5cm)
Feather pad: 20 x 20in (50 x 50cm)

See page 122 for making-up instructions

KEY TO COLOURS *(showing DMC brand
number, general colour name and number of skeins
required)*:

	7782	Gold	(6)
	7457	Dark ochre	(1)
	7303	Mid-terracotta	(5)
	7447	Dark terracotta	(13)
	7511	Dark beige	(1)
	7702	Mid-pine green	(1)
	7701	Dark pine green	(9)
	7467	Dark brown	(21)
	7535	Very dark brown	(19)
	7309	Blue-black	(5)
	7491	Light beige	(12)

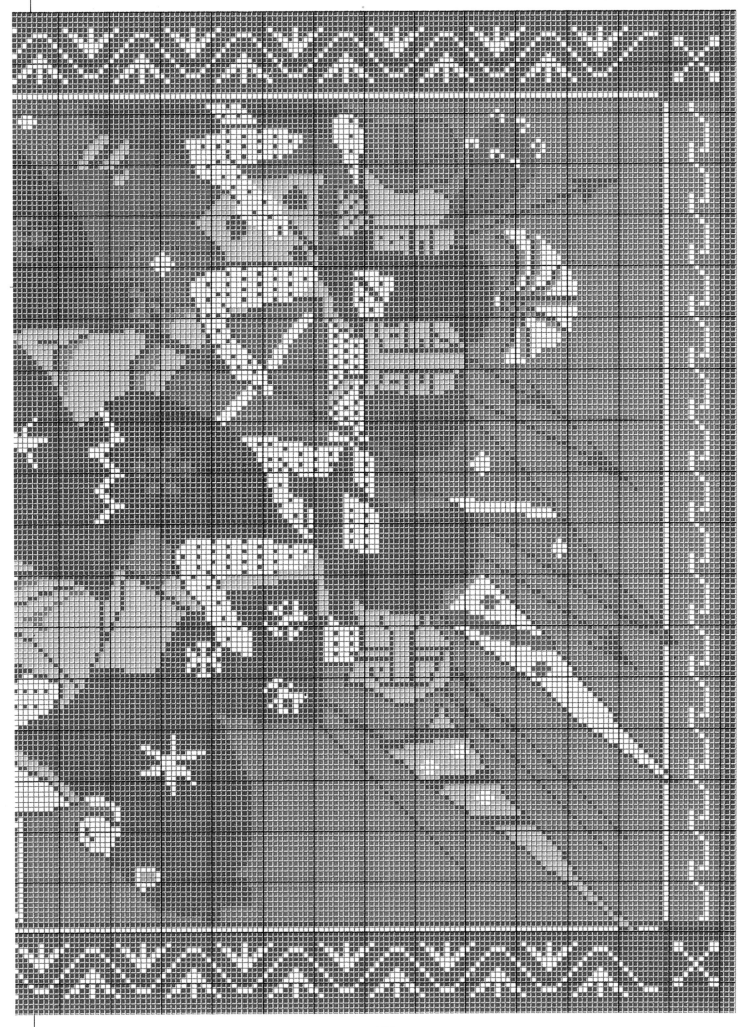

Stitching and Making-up

The Canvas

Originally made from hemp, canvas is now available in cotton, linen and silk, as well as cheaper synthetic fibres. There are two types of weave: single thread, or Mono, and double thread, or Penelope. Mono canvas is most commonly used as its simple construction makes it easier to see when counting threads. It comes in two qualities: standard and deluxe. Always use the best quality available since not only will the canvas last longer—essential when working a project which will be subject to wear and tear—but it will be kinder to the thread you are using for stitching. If in doubt, simply feel the quality of the canvas; if it has a rough texture it will snag at your thread, wearing it thin as you stitch.

Canvas comes in a wide range of sizes, and the gauge quoted under the materials needed for each project (e.g. 14-count) refers to the number of holes in the canvas per inch (2.5cm).

Needles

Use only tapestry needles for canvas work. These are blunt-ended and have large eyes. They range in size from 13 to 26—the higher the number the smaller the needle. As a general guide, size 18 is used on 10- and 12-count canvas. The rule to remember is that the eye of the needle should be very slightly larger than the hole in the canvas, so that by gently forcing the canvas threads apart it avoids the unnecessary thinning of the stitching thread. This can also be avoided by using lengths of thread that are a maximum of 18–20 inches (45–50cm) long, as anything longer will get worn away by the time it's finished, creating threadbare stitches.

It makes life easier to have a number of needles of the required size, so that you can leave them threaded up with colours which will be needed again on another part of the design.

Preparing the Canvas

Before cutting the canvas add borders of at least 2 inches (5cm) to the finished project size. As with every step of preparation and finishing, follow the weave of the canvas to create straight lines.

Fold the cut canvas in four and mark the centre point with a pin. Open out the canvas and run lines of tacking stitches along the folds to form a cross at the dead centre. This is where you will commence working.

Before starting to stitch, the raw edges of the canvas must be bound to prevent fraying and to avoid snagging your thread. If you are working without a frame or with only a simple type of frame, the edges can be covered with masking tape.

Working without a frame is not to be recommended for a number of reasons. Holding work in the hand makes tension difficult to regulate and distorts the canvas. It will also soil the work and may 'pill' the thread if handled for a long period. Most importantly, a frame facilitates stitching with an even, 'stabbing' motion. One hand remains on top of the canvas while the other stays below; the needle can then pass speedily from one side to the other, without a hand being needed to support the canvas. Using a frame with a stand also means that you can ensure you are working in a comfortable position with a good light source. Needlepoint should be a therapeutic activity, not one which results in muscle and eye strain!

STRETCHER FRAMES of the sort available in art supply shops come in specific sizes and are not adjustable. They are easy to use since the canvas may be attached directly to the wood using drawing pins or a staple gun. Start at the centre of the top edge, working outwards to the corners. Repeat along the bottom edge and then finally attach side edges. Leave a maximum of 2 inches (5cm) between tacks, to ensure that the canvas is stretched evenly and held securely.

ROLLER FRAMES come in a variety of sizes and are considered more manageable by those who prefer hand-held frames since the work is rolled up as you go, leaving only part of the design visible. The rollers have tape attached to which you stitch the top and bottom of your canvas before starting. With the basic type of roller frame it is very difficult to maintain tension without continually tightening the rollers whilst working. There is now a far more sophisticated type called 'Roll and Stretch' which allows you to lock the roller into position every time you adjust your canvas. Each frame also comes with three lengths of roller so that a variety of sizes may be accommodated. For stockists, see page 128.

SLATE FRAMES are the most traditional type of frame used for stitching purposes. They are rather time-consuming to set up since the canvas edges must be bound with webbing and then the work laced on to the frame using string. This is passed through the webbing only, using a very large needle, thus avoiding any distortion of the canvas itself.

The Stitches

TENT STITCH (OR CONTINENTAL STITCH) is probably the most commonly used stitch in needlepoint. It should not be confused with half-cross stitch, which is not recommended since it produces a fabric which lacks firmness and will not wear well. Carefully follow the numbering on diagram A, coming up on the odd numbers and going down on the even numbers. At the end of the row the stitch may be reversed, as shown in the diagram. Take great care not to split a stitch when bringing a needle up through a hole already part-filled with thread,

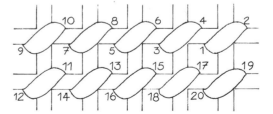

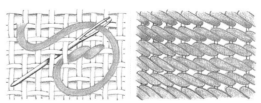

Diagram A *Tent stitch (or continental stitch):* (top) *order of stitching;* (bottom left) *front view;* (bottom right) *back view.*

since this results in stitches sitting at odd angles and creates a very uneven fabric.

Tent stitch does tend to distort the canvas and should always be worked on a frame.

DIAGONAL TENT STITCH (OR BASKETWEAVE STITCH) distorts the canvas far less than tent stitch and gives excellent coverage. Once again, follow the numbering (on diagram B), which traces the path of the thread, coming up on the odd numbers and going down on the even numbers.

On the right side of the work, the growth of the stitching is diagonal; but one look at the criss-cross pattern on the reverse side and you will understand how the stitch got its alternative name.

It should be noted that the amounts of thread quoted in this book and included in the kits listed on page 127 allow for the above stitches only. No guarantees can be given that quantities will be sufficient if other stitches are used.

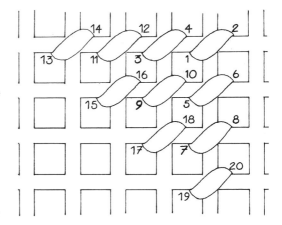

Diagram B *Diagonal tent stitch (or basketweave stitch):* (top) *order of stitching;* (bottom left) *front view;* (bottom right) *back view.*

When Working

TO START A NEW LENGTH OF THREAD (diagram C), make a knot in the end and pass it through the canvas approximately 1 inch (2.5cm) from the starting point. Now back-track over it with your first few stitches, to secure it, and then snip off the knot. Any knot that is left unsnipped may create a bump and could easily come undone.

TO FINISH OFF A THREAD (diagram D), secure it by carefully skimming the backs of several stitches, taking care not to pull them out of shape. Trim

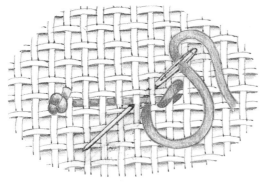

Diagram C *Starting a thread.*

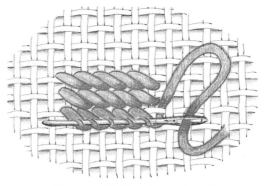

Diagram D *Finishing a thread.*

all ends, since untidy ones can easily be caught up in the stitching, causing a tangle.

Never carrying a thread for more than ½ inch (1.5cm) along the back of the work, as it can cause puckering and interfere with later stitching.

DROPPING IN SINGLE STITCHES (diagram E) is neat and easy when using an even number of strands in the needle. If working with two strands, for instance, simply use one strand, cut to double the length required. Thread both cut ends through the needle to form a loop. Work the single stitch normally but when you return the needle to the back of the work pass it through the loop. By giving it a slight tug the

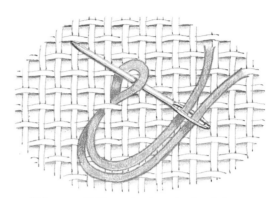

Diagram E Dropping in a single stitch.

knot becomes self-securing, and the end needs sewing in only once. This technique is very useful for correcting mistakes at a late stage.

CORRECTING MISTAKES calls for a steady hand. Never cut until you are quite sure that you are doing so in the right place, and then unpick using the end of a needle rather than continuing to cut. Remove all thread fibres from the canvas before re-stitching, so that colour areas are kept clean.

Following Charts

Each square on a chart represents one stitch; each colour, one colour of yarn, identified in the key. For clarity, the printed colour often varies from the thread colour, so you must consult the key before starting work. An overlap is indicated where a large chart is divided over two pages.

The size of each project is given, but if you would like to vary the size—making a box top into a cushion, for instance—this is done very simply by varying the gauge of the canvas used. To take an example, a design which is 140 stitches wide will stitch up to a width of 10 inches/25cm when worked on 14-count canvas ($140 \div 14 = 10$ inches/25cm). To increase the project size, the same number of stitches can be worked on a 10-count canvas ($140 \div 10 = 14$ inches/35cm). To decrease the size of the project, simply use canvas with a smaller gauge, i.e. more holes to the inch.

When changing canvas size the thickness of thread may need to be increased or decreased accordingly. It must always cover the canvas fully, without being too thick to pull easily through the holes.

Stretching the Finished Work

However neatly you may have worked your project, blocking will always improve the finish, smoothing the fabric and ensuring that it will hold its shape; for work that has become distorted it is absolutely essential.

Slightly dampen the work before you begin the stretching process as this will make it more flexible. A fine plant spray is useful for this as you need to dampen evenly but never excessively.

A piece of board which will not buckle and will take tacks or nails easily should be used for the base board. A template of the dimensions of the design can either be cut from paper and attached to the board or drawn on to the board using a waterproof pen and a set square. Using this as your guide, lay the work on to the board, face down, and tack into position, corners first.

Tacks should be placed at least 1 inch (2.5cm) from the edge of stitching in straight lines (use the threads of the canvas as guidelines) and about 1 inch (2.5cm) apart to ensure even stretching. If badly distorted, ease the work into shape as you go.

When tacked, the work should be very taut. Dampen slightly once more and leave to dry for at least thirty-six hours. Badly distorted work should be left for as long as possible, as it can easily creep out of shape again after blocking. Such work can be sized whilst stretching by evenly applying thin wallpaper paste to the reverse surface with a brush. This will help to keep it firmly in shape.

Project Finishing

CUSHIONS require backing with a fabric of a suitable shade and weight. Trim the edges of the canvas to approximately ¾ inch (2cm) from the stitching and cut across the corners diagonally to within ¼ inch (5mm) of the stitching, so that they will be sharp and square when the finished cushion is turned the right way out.

Overlock the canvas and fabric edges if you think the cushion will be taking a lot of wear and tear, and tack the backing fabric to the canvas, with reverse sides outermost. Whilst stitching the two layers together keep the canvas side uppermost, so that you can see to leave one row of stitching within the seam allowance (bare canvas should not show along the seam when the cushion is turned out). Leave a gap on the fourth side large enough to take the cushion pad. This gap can then be slip-stitched together, or a zip added if you prefer.

A small gap should also be left if the cushion is to be trimmed with braid; the cut ends of the braid can then be neatly popped into this gap and secured with a few stitches.

Use good quality pads either of roughly the same size as the design or slightly larger if you like a very plump cushion. The dining-seat pads specifically require foam pads, however, as they need to lie flat. Foam may be purchased cut to size (see page 128 for suppliers), but you will need to round off the edges so that they taper towards the seams.

Each of the pads is finished with two pieces of cord: one wrapped in a U-shape around the front and side edges, the other lying straight along the back edge, to form ties at either back corner.

TRIMMING CORD ENDS will give a much neater and more professional-looking finish to your work. Whilst working with cord or braid, a little piece of masking tape should be applied to the raw ends to stop them from fraying.

They may be finished with tag ends (see page 128 for suppliers), or with your own tassels made from matching thread.

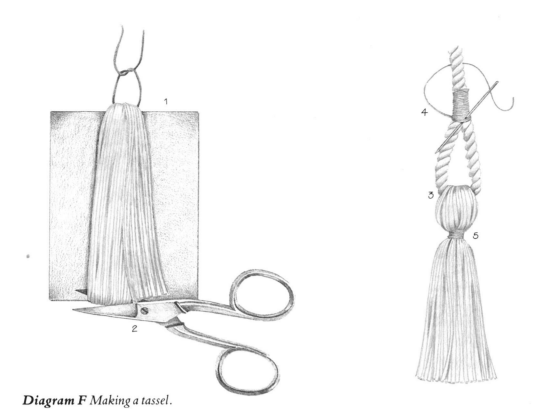

Diagram F *Making a tassel.*

TO MAKE A TASSEL (diagram F), find a stiff piece of card the appropriate depth (measurement 'A'), which should be approximately ½ inch (1.5cm) deeper than the finished tassel (the tassels on the four chair seat covers were made using a 3.5 inch (9cm) card). Taking the matching yarn, wrap it around the card quite tightly, to ensure that the strands are of a uniform length, until the tassel is as fat or thin as you require (approximately 40 wraps for the chair seat cover tassels).

Tie another piece of thread around the top of the wraps (1) to keep them together. Take some pointed scissors and cut in a straight line along the bottom of the wraps (2). Remove the cardboard, keeping the strands tidy. Pass the cord end through the wraps (3), and bind and secure the raw cord ends to the main cord (4) to form a loop. Bind the strands ½–1 inch (1.5–2.5cm) down from the top of the tassel (5), and remove the knotted thread (1). Secure as for 4, and trim the cut ends of the tassel.

THE PIN AND HERB CUSHIONS are made up in the same way as the larger cushions, but because they have curved edges, small V-shaped nicks should be made along the seam allowance to remove bulk in the finished cushions. A gap should be left in the seam to take the filling.

Bran makes a good filling for the pin cushion, while any pot-pourri, dried lavender or herb mixture may be used to fill the heart. You may prefer to contain these in a muslin bag before putting them into the cushions; ordinary stuffing can then be used around the edges to fill out the shape properly.

THE GLASSES CASE is made up like a cushion, but the top edge is left open. Using lining fabric, make another case slightly smaller than the finished case and slip it inside. Turn the top edges in on one another and stitch together.

BRAIDS give a neat finish to seam edges. Small items may be trimmed with hand-made cord (diagram G) when suitable manufactured braid is not available. By using a thread which has been used for stitching a perfect colour match is possible. The braids on the pin cushion, herb cushion and glasses case were made using 24 strands of cotton, but this method can be used for any thickness of thread.

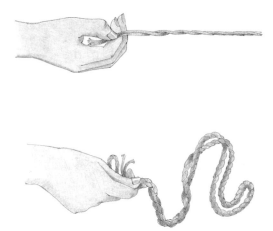

Diagram G Making braid.

Cut a length of yarn approximately four times that of the required finished measurement. Fold the yarn in half and hook the loop over a door handle. Firmly holding the two cut ends, twist the strands until they are really taut. Slip the loop off the door handle and fold the doubled strands in half. Holding the loop and cut ends in the same hand, flick the cord, allowing it to wrap around itself. Gently smooth it out with your fingers so that the twist is even along its length, and tie the loop and cut ends together. The cord can now be invisibly stitched on to the project using a single strand of the same thread.

THE WORK-BOX TOP, PENCIL BOX AND FOOTSTOOL all use manufactured furniture bases which come supplied with detachable pads for covering (details of suppliers on page 128). Fit the canvas over the pad and tape it on to the supporting board behind, to keep it in position. The corners should be clipped across diagonally and loosely eased over the pad corners so that they are neat and smooth. Only when perfectly positioned should the canvas border be stapled down to the board; place the staples close together to exert an even pressure on the canvas. The finished upholstered pad should then be dropped into its base frame and screwed down.

THE FRAMED PANELS AND FIRESCREEN were professionally finished, but if you want to tackle framing yourself it is first necessary to mount the work on very stiff card (diagram H). Strong buttonthread is ideal for this task, and by leaving it attached to the reel and lacing in the manner shown, the tension may be adjusted easily.

Since the finished project must lie absolutely flat, attention should be paid to properly mitring the corners. First cut across them diagonally to within ¼ inch (5mm) of the stitching edge. Turn over the ¼ inch (5mm) strip first and then turn down the sides of the work. The mitre can then be stitched, as shown, to hold it in place. Once all four corners have been mitred, the other two sides can be laced together.

THE PICTURE FRAME project may be tackled in much the same manner. Trim the canvas into a frame shape, leaving ½ inch (1.5cm) of canvas around the inner and outer edges. With a sharp knife and a metal ruler, cut a very thick piece of card to the size of the frame, allowing for one row of stitching around the outer edge of the canvas to overlap on to the underside of the card. Snip the inner corners, mitre the outer ones (diagram H) and neatly fold the work around the card. Lace together, taking the needle through the canvas quite close to the stitching. Take another piece of card, which is slightly thicker than the mirror or picture that you intend to use, and cut it to the same shape as the frame but ⅛ inch (3mm) narrower on both edges. Glue it centrally to the back of the frame, and drop in your mirror or mounted picture and glass, holding it in position with strong pins knocked into the sides of the card. Cut a piece of non-fraying fabric, such as felt, a fraction smaller than the finished frame and stitch it on to the line of stitches overlapping on to the back of the card. For a free-standing frame, a card stand may be glued to the back.

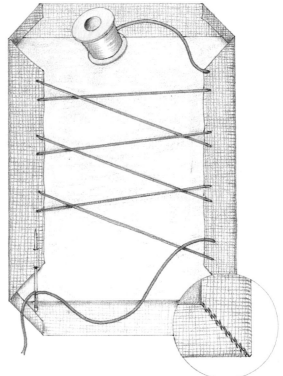

Diagram H *Mounting: lacing and mitring corners.*

THE BELL-PULL AND HANGING, which simply need backing, must be blocked especially carefully so that they will hang squarely. The selvedges should be turned under, mitred (diagram H) and pressed.

To give extra body, interlining of an appropriate thickness should be added at this stage. (If it is not self-adhesive use strips of dressmaker's adhesive webbing or stitch it in place.)

If hanging loops are to be used, these should be stitched into position before the backing fabric is attached. Use a non-fraying fabric, such as felt, or turn in the edges of a woven fabric before sewing it on to the back of the project. Once again, there are self-adhesive varieties available.

If a rod is to be used, turn the backing fabric under to create a tube along the top edge, running a line of stitching across it before sewing it to the canvas. Leave the ends along the side seam open.

Should you wish to hang it like a picture, simply attach a lightweight wooden baton to the back of the completed work and afix small picture-hanging screws and hanging wire.

THE PELMET AND TIE-BACKS should be backed as described above. So that you may attach the pelmet wherever you please, and to facilitate cleaning, use heavyweight sticky-backed Velcro for mounting. Stick one side of the Velcro to the backed pelmet and the other to an existing pelmet or a baton attached to the wall.

The tie-backs can be fastened to fixings on the wall with extensions of the braid used for edging them. Alternatively, braid loops may be made at the ends or ornamental rings added, both of which will then simply slip over a hook on the wall.

THE RUG must be blocked extremely carefully since the panels must square up to one another and be exactly the same size. Stitch them together, end to end in threes, to make two strips. Press the seams open, trim the inner corners, then stitch the two strips together.

If you wish to add a fringe, leave one row of canvas just visible when you come to fold in the top and bottom edges of the rug (this will be hidden when the fringe is attached).

To make the fringe (diagram I), cut a strip of card 2 inches (5cm) deeper than the length of the fringe required. Wrap your thread evenly around the card, and cut the wraps along one edge. Take a single strand, fold it in half and thread a large tapestry needle with the loop end. Pass the needle through a hole in the canvas, from front to back, remove the needle, slip the cut ends through the loop and tighten up the knot. Work a fringe into every other hole all along the edge. Finally, comb and trim ends and back the rug.

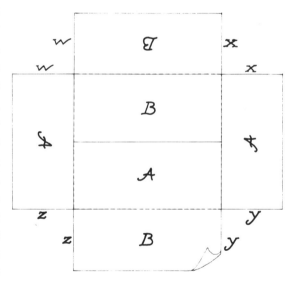

Diagram I *Making a fringe.*

THE BOX STOOL needs to be worked in a cross shape, with the panels placed as shown on the flat-plan (diagram J). If this is too cumbersome, work the side panels separately and join them to the top before sewing up the corner seams. The panels should be placed in the direction of the letters on the plan, and all stitching should be worked in the same direction. Trim away excess canvas and join the corner seams (matching W to W, X to X, etc.). Trim the corners to within ¼ inch (5mm) of the stitching, and turn the canvas the right way out to form the box shape. Drop this over the ready-made padded stool (see page 128 for suppliers), turn borders under and staple to the bottom of the stool. Cover with backing fabric.

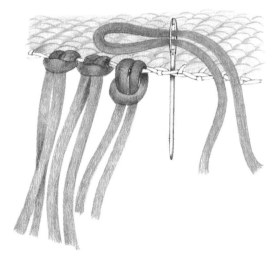

Diagram J *Box stool flat-plan.*